Preservation Management of Digital Materials
A Handbook

By Maggie Jones and Neil Beagrie

For Resource: The Council for Museums, Archives and Libraries

THE BRITISH LIBRARY

First Published 2001 by
The British Library
96 Euston Road
London
NWI 2DB

Reprinted with corrections 2003

British Library Cataloguing in Publication Data
A CIP record is available from The British Library

ISBN 0-7123-0886-5

Designed and typeset by Julie Rimmer
Printed in England by Hobbs the Printers Ltd, Totton, Hampshire SO40 3YS

Contents

List of Figures

The handbook was initially made possible through funding allocated by the Library and Information Commission (subsequently Resource). This has been supplemented by contributions from the Arts and Humanities Data Service (AHDS) and the Joint Information Systems Committee (JISC) Digital Preservation Focus whose staff made the original proposal and undertook the research, writing and administrative work. The contribution of the Advisory Group, some of whom have spent significant amounts of time in reviewing the handbook, has done much to improve the handbook and to provide overall guidance for the project. The Case Study interviewees at the British Library, University of Hull and the Royal Commission on the Ancient and Historical Monuments of Scotland contributed much time and effort in preparing for, and undertaking, interviews. Some also provided valuable feedback to the handbook to help ensure its practical relevance. Last, but not least, the specialist interviewees and peer review respondents gave generously of their time and provided additional insights based on their expertise and experience. Further practical testing and implementation of the handbook in draft form was also made possible by a grant from the British Library Co-operation and Partnership Programme and the participation of staff from the British Library, Cambridge University and the University of Oxford. The time and effort of all who have participated in the project is gratefully acknowledged.

Project Team
Neil Beagrie (Project Director), Maggie Jones (Research), Eileen Boyce and Louise Heath (Administration and Secretarial Support), Dan Greenstein (Director AHDS to November 1999).

Advisory Group
Sheila Anderson (Essex Data Archive), Kevin Ashley (University of London Computing Centre), Charles Dollar (Charles Dollar & Associates), Nancy Elkington (Research Libraries Group), Helen Forde (Public Record Office) Daniel Greenstein (Digital Library Federation), Alison Horsburgh (National Archives of Scotland), Stuart Lee (University of Oxford), Vanessa Marshall (National Preservation Office), Simon Matty (Re:source), Seamus Ross (HATII University of Glasgow), Chris Rusbridge (JISC later University of Glasgow), Kelly Russell (Cedars University of Leeds), Helen Shenton (British Library).

Case Study Interviewees
British Library: Michael Alexander, Stephen Andrews, John Fletcher, John Hopson, Graham Jefcoate, Crispin Jewitt, Ed King, David Inglis, Dennis Pilling, Geoff Smith, Kate Streatfield, Susan Whitfield.
University of Hull: Glenn Burgess, Penny Grubb, John Chipperfield, Bruce Pears, Bridget Towler.
Royal Commission on Ancient and Historical Manuscripts of Scotland: Lesley Ferguson, Ian Fraser, Mark Gillick, John Keggie, Diana Murray, Ian Parker.

Specialist Interviewees
Chris Batt (Resource); Richard Blake (Public Record Office); Ann Hughes (Joint Information Systems Committee); Derek Law (University of Strathclyde); Philip Lord (Smith Kline Beecham); Cliff Morgan (John Wiley & Sons); Dennis Nicholson (University of Strathclyde).

Other Peer Review Respondents
Helen Baigent (Resource), Christine Dugdale (University of the West of England), Luciana Duranti (University of British Columbia), Anne Gilliland-Swetland (University of California Los Angeles), Susan Hockey (University College London), Alan Howell (State Library of Victoria), Hamish James (History Data Service), Greg Lawrence (University of Cornell), Oya Rieger (University of Cornell), Colin Webb (National Library of Australia), Michael Wettengel (Bundesarchiv).

Neil Beagrie took up his appointment as an Assistant Director in the DNER Office of the Joint Information Systems Committee in June 2000. He is responsible for the activities of JISC Digital Preservation Focus. He was previously Assistant Director of the Arts and Humanities Data Service. At the AHDS he was responsible for digital collections policy and standards development and published extensively on digital preservation issues. He was joint author with Daniel Greenstein of the LIC funded study "A Strategic Policy Framework for Creating and Preserving Digital Collections". Prior to joining the AHDS in 1997, he was Head of Archaeological Archives and Library at the Royal Commission on the Historical Monuments of England.

Maggie Jones has been working for the Arts and Humanities Data Service since July 1999. Before returning to the UK in 1998 she worked at the National Library of Australia for seventeen years. Her last position at the NLA was Director of Collection Management and Retrieval Services which combined the preservation of the Library's collections, and the stack retrieval service. She became very interested in the preservation of digital materials during this time and was one of the founder members of the PADI (Preserving Access to Digital Information) working group.

1. INTRODUCTION

1.1 Background

There is a rapidly increasing volume of information which exists in digital form. Whether created as a result of digitising non-digital collections, created as a digital publication, or created as part of the day-to-day business of an organisation, more and more information is being created digitally and the pace at which it is being created is accelerating. In the UK, initiatives such as the People's Network and the National Grid for Learning have emerged with a consequent need for quality digital materials to support them. Numerous other digitisation initiatives either planned or underway are constantly being announced within the commercial, higher education, and public sectors. In addition, a Government white paper announced the intention to have all newly created public records electronically stored and retrieved by 2004[1].

This activity is occurring in an environment in which there is a growing awareness of the significant challenges associated with ensuring continued access to these materials, even in the short term. In the UK, a series of research reports were commissioned by JISC (Joint Information Systems Committee) and the NPO (National Preservation Office) which served to highlight various aspects of digital preservation[2]. The reports provided a broad overview of key issues and two in particular (Beagrie and Greenstein[3] and Hendley[4]) recommended that further research be undertaken to explore the issues they raised in more detail.

The combination of these two factors is both challenging and troublesome. On the one hand, there are considerable opportunities offered by digital technology to provide rapid and efficient access to information. On the other hand, there is a very real threat that the digital materials will be created in such a way that not even their short-term viability can be assured, much less the prospect that future generations will also have access to them. The need to create and have widespread access to digital materials has raced ahead of the level of general awareness and understanding of what it takes to manage them effectively.

The need for guidance

Both the JISC/NPO studies and the second workshop in digital preservation organised by the JISC and the British Library in 1999 at Warwick identified the need to improve guidance on digital preservation. At around the same time, a survey commissioned by RLG (Research Libraries Group) investigated the needs of member institutions[5]. A clear picture emerged from both sets of activities of a complex and rapidly changing environment in which those creating and/or acquiring digital resources would require guidance on how to manage those resources most effectively.

1

All organisations in all sectors have been or will soon be creating digital materials. They may be created as part of their organisational records, they may be created by digitising non-digital collections in order to enhance access to them, or they may be created digitally ("born digital"). However, they come into being, they will need to be managed as early as possible in their life-cycle, preferably at the design stage, but if not as soon as practicable thereafter, if they are to remain accessible as long as they are required. Practical experience and expertise in this area is still scarce so there is a clear need for guidance to ensure that the significant opportunities are not overwhelmed by the equally significant threats.

Given this conjunction of factors, it seemed timely to embark on a handbook which aimed at both identifying good practice in creating and managing and preserving digital materials and also providing a range of practical tools to assist in that process. This handbook is being produced at a time when an important body of experience is emerging from recent research projects into digital preservation and from established data archives in the sciences and social sciences. Although many challenges remain, it is now possible to point to many examples of good practice and to suggest ways in which institutions can begin to address digital preservation. By providing a strategic overview of the key issues, discussion and guidance on strategies and activities, and pointers to key projects and reports, the handbook aims to provide guidance for institutions and individuals and a range of tools to help them identify and take appropriate actions.

Development of the handbook

In 1999 the AHDS (Arts and Humanities Data Service) submitted a proposal to the Preservation of and Access to the Recorded Heritage Research Programme. The proposal aimed to build on work which has already taken place in identifying the broad issues and challenges associated with digital preservation, and to provide more detailed guidance to all those creating and/or acquiring digital materials. The AHDS has considerable experience in collecting and managing digital materials and has been active in providing guidance in creating digital materials for the arts and humanities. Many of the challenges associated with ensuring continued access to digital materials are identical regardless of how or where they are created, so it made sense to build on this practical experience and to aim at a wider audience. The project was awarded funding of £33,561 from Resource: The Council for Museums, Archives and Libraries, with contributing in kind funding from AHDS and JISC, institutions represented by the Advisory Group, and participating case studies. The work was undertaken between July 1999 and September 2000 by Neil Beagrie and Maggie Jones on behalf of the AHDS.

An Advisory Group consisting of experts in the field of digital preservation was formed, all of whom had first hand knowledge of the range of complex issues involved. An early decision was that a handbook would be the most appropriate mechanism to provide the range of advice and guidance required for such a diverse audience. Research to compile the handbook combined traditional desktop research, utilising the world-wide-web as a source of freely available current information, as well as subscription-based print and electronic journals, supplemented with case studies and specialist interviews. Three very different case studies were selected to help develop the practical nature of the handbook and to ensure that it addressed key issues currently being faced by organisations. Through structured interviews with selected specialists, workshops and conference presentations, and the case studies, it was possible to gauge the overall level of awareness and understanding of digital preservation and to transfer that knowledge to the development of the handbook.

A consultation period for peer review and assessment was provided between 8 August and 4 September 2000. Comments were also accepted up until the end of the project to allow those wishing to comment to do so.

In general, the research for the handbook showed that the level of awareness of, and interest in, digital preservation is gradually increasing but is not keeping pace with the level of digital resource creation. In particular, institutions that have not played a role in preserving traditional collections do not have a strong sense of playing a role in preserving digital materials. Individual researchers were keen to "do the right thing" but frequently lacked the clear guidance and institutional backing to enable them to feel confident of what they should be doing. The difficulties of allocating responsibilities for preservation and maintenance in an environment in which digital resource creation is frequently a by-product of collaborative projects, which may well be funded by yet another external agency, was also mentioned. Overall, it appears that there is still a need to raise the level of awareness of digital preservation, particularly among funding agencies and senior administrators with responsibility for the strategic direction of an institution. This needs to be combined with more detailed guidance and training at the operational level. Moreover, the guidance needs to be able to accommodate people with varying levels of awareness and understanding of digital preservation, in a wide range of institutional settings, all of whose staff have significant constraints on their time.

Audience and purpose

Digital preservation has many parallels with traditional preservation in matters of broad principle but differs markedly at the operational level and never more so than in the wide range of decision makers who play a crucial role at various stages in the lifecycle of a digital resource. Consequently, this handbook is aiming at a very broad audience. In the first instance it is intended to provide guidance to institutions at national, regional and local levels who are involved in or contemplating creation and/or acquisition of digital materials. Within those institutions, the handbook is aiming at both administrators and practitioners and is accordingly structured to include a mix of high level strategic overviews and detailed guidance. In addition, the handbook is aimed at service providers who may be in a position to provide all or part of the services needed to preserve digital materials. It is also relevant to funding agencies who will need to be aware of the implications of the creation of digital materials. Finally, it will be of interest to data creators whose involvement in the preservation of their digital materials is still crucial, despite being restricted by the overarching business needs of their organisation.

The handbook fully recognises that these groups may have different interests and involvement with digital materials at different times. By adopting the life-cycle approach to digital preservation it aims to help identify dependencies, barriers, and mechanisms to assist communication and collaboration between these communities.

The need to tailor the handbook to the needs of individual institutions, including those where digital preservation may be outsourced and those where digital preservation may only be short-term, means that the handbook needs to be seen as acting as a catalyst for further concerted action within and between institutions.

The broad issues associated with digital preservation are global in nature and examples of good practice, research activity and sources of advice and guidance have been drawn from around the world. However, there is a UK focus in terms of the background to the study and some examples, e.g. legislation, are UK specific. The text of the handbook will indicate a UK focus whenever relevant. It is still hoped that the handbook will be relevant to an international audience as many of the models and references provided are not UK based and are in any case applicable to any country. Wherever their country of origin, the users of the handbook will need to tailor it to their specific needs.

The overall theme of the handbook is that while the issues are complex and much remains to be clarified (and may never be definitively resolved), there is nevertheless much that has already been achieved and much that can be undertaken immediately by all involved in creating and/or acquiring digital materials. This activity will help to protect the initial investment in digital materials creation and offer considerably improved prospects for the long-term.

Web version of the handbook

In such a rapidly developing environment, it will clearly be necessary to maintain the handbook to ensure its currency. This will be achieved by having an electronic version and supporting materials available on the Digital Preservation Coalition website, which will be updated on a regular basis to ensure currency of web references and cited projects. This print publication provides a convenient reference work which will be complemented and supported by the web version. Users of the print version should consult the Digital Preservation Coalition website regularly for current urls and future updates. The web version will be available from:
<http://www.dpconline.org>

Future development and support

The development of the handbook to date has been the result of collaboration and input from a wide range of institutions and individuals. We hope the momentum and focus for future development and maintenance of the handbook will be created by the establishment of the Digital Preservation Coalition in 2001. This will provide the opportunity to link the handbook to supporting materials and training workshops and to add further case studies and exemplars as experience and practice in digital preservation grows. Further details will be linked from the web version of the handbook.

The authors welcome feedback and constructive suggestions for improving the handbook. Please send comments to:

Email: preservation@jisc.ac.uk
Mail: JISC Digital Preservation Focus, JISC Office, King's College London, Strand Bridge House, 138-142 The Strand, London WC2R 1HH

Introduction

References

1. Modernising Government. March 1999. Cm 4310. Chapter 5.
    <http://www.official-documents.co.uk/document/cm43/4310/4310.htm>
    Also available as a PDF file at:
    <http://cabinet-office.gov.uk/moderngov/download/modgov.pdf>

2. The seven commissioned reports are available at the UKOLN website
    <http://www.ukoln.ac.uk/services/elib/papers/supporting>

3. Beagrie, N. and Greenstein, D. (1998). A Strategic Policy Framework for
    Creating and Preserving Digital Collections. Version 4.0 (Final Draft). ELib
    Supporting Study p3. Library Information and Technology Centre, South
    Bank University, London.
    <http://ahds.ac.uk/strategic.htm>

4. Hendley, T. (1998). Comparison of Methods and Costs of Digital
    Preservation. British Library Research and Innovation Report 109.
    London: the British Library.
    <http://www.ukoln.ac.uk/services/elib/papers/tavistock/hendley/hendley.html>

5. Hedstrom, M. and Montgomery, S. (1998). Digital Preservation Needs and
    Requirements in RLG Member Institutions. Mountain View CA: RLG.
    <http://www.rlg.ac.uk/preserv/digpres.html>

Introduction

1.2 How to Use the Handbook

The needs of institutions regarding the digital materials they create and acquire vary considerably. This handbook is intended to provide a bridge between broad, high level overviews and explicit, detailed guidelines applicable to the needs of a specific institution. The strategic overviews are intended to link to operational activities in order to reinforce the need to develop practical procedures grounded firmly in the business mission of the institution. The handbook provides pointers to where to find further guidance and to assist in developing policies and practices which are most applicable to the individual institution.

Ideally, the handbook should be used as a mechanism to help focus thoughts, increase overall understanding, promote training, and act as a catalyst for further action. Nothing will preclude the need for each organisation ultimately to commit the necessary resources to an action plan but this handbook is intended to oil the wheels of that process. While the challenges may seem daunting initially, the overall message of the handbook is that it is possible to take action now, and to make significant progress towards developing the infrastructure that will greatly improve future prospects for quality digital materials being created at this time. It is neither possible nor necessary to wait until all challenges have been overcome before action is taken. Nor is it necessary to wait until the long-term costs are clearly known. It is often never known precisely how much it costs to preserve traditional collections nor has it been necessary to resolve every obstacle definitively before developing effective preservation programmes.

If, as seems clear, society is to rely on assured access to digital as well as non-digital sources of information, then the ways and means of providing assured and continued access must be found.

A range of tools has been used in the handbook, both because of the inconsistent level of existing guidance and also the range of user needs. For some aspects, such as digital imaging, there are numerous excellent sources of practical guidance, while other operational requirements are less fully developed at this stage. All can be expected to change and evolve fairly rapidly so the handbook is advocating an overall approach to preserving digital resources based on sound principles and policies rather than prescriptive formulae. As the crucial importance of digital preservation becomes more widely recognised, an increasing number of valuable sources of guidance are appearing at a rapid rate. While potentially incredibly valuable, their proliferation can make it bewildering to decide which ones are likely to be most applicable for a given situation.

By selecting key exemplars and further reading in each section, the handbook should make it easier to navigate through existing sources of advice, guidance and options. In addition to pointing to existing sources of guidance, a combination of decision tree, summary checklists, selected case studies, and commentary have been used. These are intended to stimulate and promote further thought and discussion but above all, to stimulate action by institutions to develop digital preservation management policies and strategies appropriate to their needs.

The handbook is intended for a wide and diverse audience, from those who are only beginning to consider managing digital materials to practitioners who have already accumulated considerable theoretical and/or practical experience. It has been written with the intention of allowing quick and easy access to the most appropriate chapters.

Each chapter is preceded by an 'at a glance' guide to its intended primary audience, their assumed level of knowledge, and the purpose of the chapter. The table below is intended to help in deciding which chapters are likely to be of most relevance. It is however not intended to be rigidly prescriptive and anyone wishing to, can of course read the handbook in its entirety!

All readers are encouraged to read Chapter 1, which provides the background to the development of the handbook and guidance on how it is to be used. A set of definitions and concise explanations of key concepts is provided in **1.3** and a glossary of acronyms and initials use by organisations and projects throughout the handbook is provided in **1.4** of the Introduction. Finally a topic index at the back of the handbook allows readers to identify and locate key subjects covered.

Figure 1
Recommended Chapters and Audiences

Audience	Recommended Chapters
Anyone requiring an introduction to the subject	Chapter two
Creators and publishers	Chapters two, four and five
Funding agencies	Chapter two
Operational managers	Chapters three, four and five
Operational staff	Chapters four and five
Senior administrators	Chapter three
Third party service providers	Chapters three, four and five

1.3 Definitions and Concepts

Introduction

A major difficulty in any newly emerging discipline, such as digital preservation, is the lack of a precise and definitive taxonomy of terms. Different communities use the same terms in different ways which can make effective communication problematic. The following working set of definitions are those used throughout the handbook and are intended to assist in its use as a practical tool. These definitions will not necessarily achieve widespread consensus among the wide ranging communities the handbook is aiming at, they are offered here as a mechanism to avoid potential ambiguities in the body of the handbook rather than as a definitive gloss. Where they have been taken from existing glossaries, this has been acknowledged.

Access As defined in the handbook, access is assumed to mean continued, ongoing usability of a digital resource, retaining all qualities of authenticity, accuracy and functionality deemed to be essential for the purposes the digital material was created and/or acquired for.

Authentication A mechanism which attempts to establish the authenticity of digital materials at a particular point in time. For example, digital signatures.

Authenticity The digital material is what it purports to be. In the case of electronic records, it refers to the trustworthiness of the electronic record as a record. In the case of "born digital" and digitised materials, it refers to the fact that whatever is being cited is the same as it was when it was first created unless the accompanying metadata indicates any changes. Confidence in the authenticity of digital materials over time is particularly crucial owing to the ease with which alterations can be made.

"Born Digital" Digital materials which are not intended to have an analogue equivalent, either as the originating source or as a result of conversion to analogue form. This term has been used in the handbook to differentiate them from 1) digital materials which have been created as a result of converting analogue originals; and 2) digital materials, which may have originated from a digital source but have been printed to paper, e.g. some electronic records.

Digital Archiving This term is used very differently within sectors. The library and archiving communities often use it interchangeably with digital preservation. Computing professionals tend to use digital archiving to mean the process of backup and ongoing maintenance as opposed to strategies for long-term digital preservation. It is this latter richer definition, as defined under digital preservation which has been used throughout this handbook.

Digital Materials A broad term encompassing digital surrogates created as a result of converting analogue materials to digital form (digitisation), and "born digital" for which there has never been and is never intended to be an analogue equivalent, and digital records.

Digital Preservation Refers to the series of managed activities necessary to ensure continued access to digital materials for as long as necessary. Digital preservation is defined very broadly for the purposes of this study and refers to all of the actions required to maintain access to digital materials beyond the limits of media failure or technological change. Those materials may be records created during the day-to-day business of an organisation; "born-digital" materials created for a specific purpose (e.g. teaching resources); or the products of digitisation projects. This handbook specifically excludes the potential use of digital technology to preserve the original artefacts through digitisation. See also Digitisation definition below.

- Long-term preservation – Continued access to digital materials, or at least to the information contained in them, indefinitely.
- Medium-term preservation – Continued access to digital materials beyond changes in technology for a defined period of time but not indefinitely.
- Short-term preservation – Access to digital materials either for a defined period of time while use is predicted but which does not extend beyond the foreseeable future and/or until it becomes inaccessible because of changes in technology.

Digital Publications "Born digital" objects which have been released for public access and either made available or distributed free of charge or for a fee. They may consist of networked publications, available over a communications network or physical format publications which are distributed on formats such as floppy or optical disks. They may also be either static or dynamic.

Digital Records See Electronic Records

Digital Resources See Digital Materials

Digitisation The process of creating digital files by scanning or otherwise converting analogue materials. The resulting digital copy, or digital surrogate, would then be classed as digital material and then subject to the same broad challenges involved in preserving access to it, as "born digital" materials.

Documentation The information provided by a creator and the repository which provides enough information to establish provenance, history and context and to enable its use by others. See also Metadata (page 11). "At a minimum, documentation should provide information about a data collection's contents, provenance and structure, and the terms and conditions that apply to its use. It needs to be sufficiently detailed to allow the data creator to use the material in the future, when the data creation process has started to fade from memory. It also needs to be comprehensive enough to enable others to explore the resource fully, and detailed enough to allow someone who has not been involved in the data creation process to understand the data collection and the process by which it was created." [1]

Electronic Records Records created digitally in the day-to-day business of the organisation and assigned formal status by the organisation. They may include for example, word processing documents, emails, databases, or intranet web pages.

Emulation A means of overcoming technological obsolescence of hardware and software by developing techniques for imitating obsolete systems on future generations of computers.

Life-cycle Management Records management practices have established life-cycle management for many years, for both paper and electronic records. The major implications for life-cycle management of digital resources, whatever their form or function, is the need actively to manage the resource at each stage of its life-cycle and to recognise the inter-dependencies between each stage and commence preservation activities as early as practicable. This represents a major difference with most traditional preservation, where management is largely passive until detailed conservation work is required, typically, many years after creation and rarely, if ever, involving the creator. There is an active and inter-linked life-cycle to digital resources which has prompted many to promote the term "continuum" to distinguish it from the more traditional and linear flow of the life-cycle for traditional analogue materials. We have used the term life-cycle to apply to this pro-active concept of preservation management for digital materials. The rationale for this approach is summed up in the following quotations:
"…the prospects for and the costs involved in preserving digital resources over the longer term rest heavily upon decisions taken about those resources at different stages of their life cycle. Decisions taken in the design and creation of a digital resource, and those taken when a digital resource is accessioned into a collection, are particularly influential." [2]
"At each phase of the cycle, electronic records need to be actively managed, according to established procedures, to ensure that they retain qualities of integrity, authenticity and reliability." [3]

Metadata Information which describes significant aspects of a resource. Most discussion to date has tended to emphasise metadata for the purposes of resource discovery. The emphasis in this handbook is on what metadata are required successfully to manage and preserve digital materials over time and which will assist in ensuring essential contextual, historical, and technical information are preserved along with the digital object.

Migration A means of overcoming technological obsolescence by transferring digital resources from one hardware/software generation to the next. The purpose of migration is to preserve the intellectual content of digital objects and to retain the ability for clients to retrieve, display, and otherwise use them in the face of constantly changing technology. Migration differs from the refreshing of storage media in that it is not always possible to make an exact digital copy or replicate original features and appearance and still maintain the compatibility of the resource with the new generation of technology.

Reformatting Copying information content from one storage medium to a different storage medium (media reformatting) or converting from one file format to a different file format (file re-formatting).

Refreshing Copying information content from one storage media to the same storage media.

References

1. History Data Service. Guideline for Depositors.
   <http://hds.essex.ac.uk/depguide.asp>

2. Beagrie, N. and Greenstein, D. (1998). A Strategic Policy Framework for Creating and Preserving Digital Collections. Version 4.0 (Final Draft). ELib Supporting Study p3. Library Information and Technology Centre, South Bank University, London. p. 3.
   <http://ahds.ac.uk/strategic.htm>

3. PRO. (1999). Management, Appraisal and Preservation of Electronic Records. Volume 1: Principles. p. 37.
   <http://www.pro.gov.uk/recordsmanagement/eros/guidelines>

Introduction

1.4 Acronyms and Initials

ADS Archaeology Data Service
<http://ads.ahds.ac.uk>

AHDS Arts and Humanities Data Service
<http://ahds.ac.uk>

CAMiLEON Creative Archiving at Michigan & Leeds: Emulating the Old on the New <http://www.si.umich.edu/CAMILEON>

Cedars CURL Exemplars in Digital Archiving
<http://www.leeds.ac.uk/cedars>

CLIR Council on Library and Information Resources
<http://www.clir.org>

CNI Coalition for Networked Information
<http://www.cni.org>

CURL Consortium of University Research Libraries
<http://www.curl.ac.uk>

DDI Data Documentation Initiative
<http://www.icpsr.umich.edu/DDI/codebook/codedtd.html>

DLF Digital Library Federation
<http://www.clir.org/diglib>

ECUP European Copyright User Platform
<http://www.eblida.org/ecup>

EPIC European Preservation Information Centre
<http://www.knaw.nl/ecpa>

EROS Electronic Records in Office Systems
<http://pro.gov.uk/recordsmanagement/eros.default.htm>

HDS History Data Service
<http://hds.essex.ac.uk>

HEDS Higher Education Digitisation Service
<http://heds.herts.ac.uk>

InterPARES project International Research on Permanent Authentic Records in Electronic Systems
<http://www.interpares.org>

JISC Joint Information Systems Committee of the Higher and Further Education Councils
<http://www.jisc.ac.uk>

NDAD UK National Digital Archive of Datasets
<http://www.pro.gov.uk/recordsmanagement/uknda>

NEDLIB Networked European Deposit Library
<http://www.konbib.nl/nedlib>

NESLI National Electronic Site Licensing Initiative
<http://www.nesli.ac.uk>

NGfL National Grid for Learning
<http://www.ngfl.gov.uk>

NML National Media Laboratory (United States)
<http://www.nml.org>

NOF New Opportunities Fund
<http://www.nof.org.uk>
and
<http://www.peoplesnetwork.gov.uk/nof/index.html>

NPO National Preservation Office
<http://www.bl.uk/services/preservation>

OAIS Open Archival Information System
<http://ssdoo.gsfc.nasa.gov/nost/isoas/overview.html>

OCLC Online Computer Library Center
<http://www.oclc.org/home>

OTA Oxford Text Archive
<http://ota.ahds.ac.uk>

PADI Preserving Access to Digital Information
<http://www.nla.gov.au/padi>

PADS Performing Arts Data Service
<http://www.pads.ahds.ac.uk>

PANDORA Preserving and Accessing Networked Documentary Resources of Australia
<http://pandora.nla.gov.au>

PRISM Project Preservation, Reliability, Interoperability, Security, Metadata
<http://www.prism.cornell.edu/main.htm>

PRO Public Record Office
<http://www.pro.gov.uk>

PURL Persistent Uniform Resource Locator
<http://purl.nla.gov.au>

RLG Research Libraries Group
<http://www.rlg.ac.uk>

TASI Technical Advisory Service for Images
<http://www.tasi.ac.uk>

UKOLN UK Office for Library and Information Networking
<http://www.ukoln.ac.uk>

ULCC University of London Computer Centre
<http://www.ulcc.ac.uk>

VADS Visual Arts Data Service
<http://vads.ahds.ac.uk>

2. Digital Preservation

Intended primary audience

Senior administrators, funding agencies, creators and publishers, anyone requiring an introduction to the subject.

Assumed level of knowledge of digital preservation

Novice.

Purpose

- To provide a strategic overview and senior management briefing, outlining the broad issues and the rationale for funding to be allocated to the tasks involved in preserving digital resources.
- To provide a synthesis of current thinking on digital preservation issues.
- To distinguish between the three major categories of issues.
- To help clarify how various issues will impact on decisions at various stages of the life-cycle of digital materials.
- To provide a focus for further debate and discussion within organisations.

2.1 Strategic Overview

- **Why** is it necessary to take action?
- **How** are digital materials different?
- **What** digital materials are being produced?
- **Who** needs to be involved?
- **How** much does it cost?

Why is it necessary to take action?

More and more information is being created in digital form, either through converting existing materials to digital form or, increasingly, "born digital", where there is no other format but the digital original. There are increasing expectations in all spheres of life that the information we all need will be available on the Internet or at least in an offline digital format, such as CD-ROM. Digital access has many advantages over paper-based or microform access in terms of convenience and functionality. The increasing proliferation of digital information, combined with the considerable challenges, detailed elsewhere in this handbook, associated with ensuring continued access to digital information, means that it is imperative that there be concerted action to overcome these challenges. While there is as yet only largely anecdotal evidence, it is certain that many potentially valuable digital materials have already been lost. Some of these may have disappeared without ever having reached a wider audience than the original creators[1]. At the very least, this constitutes failure fully to maximise the potential benefits of the investment expended in creating these digital materials.

In 1996, a specially commissioned US Taskforce on Digital Archiving published the final report of its work[2]. The impact of the work of the Taskforce has been felt world-wide. In the UK, it was a key influence in a workshop sponsored by the Joint Information Systems Committee (JISC) and the British Library[3].

The implications for preserving continued access to important digital materials is already being felt by libraries and archives, many of which have begun to consider and take initial steps to meet their responsibility effectively. As business records are increasingly being created digitally records managers in the commercial sector and government also need to consider how they will implement records management practices which will ensure continued access to important digital records. In addition, the museums and cultural heritage sectors are increasingly utilising digital technology to create digital surrogates of rare, unique and valuable collections. The primary objective of these projects is invariably access. Preservation considerations, if they are stated at all, tend to be primarily related to the preservation of the object being digitised, not to the digital surrogate. However, a logical consequence which very quickly becomes apparent, is the question of how long access to the digital surrogate can be maintained. If access cannot be maintained beyond the short-term, then how can the initial (and often substantial) investment in creating the digital resources be justified?

How are digital materials different?

As a recent Research Libraries Group (RLG) Survey noted:
"Digital materials, regardless of whether they are created initially in digital form or converted to digital form, are threatened by technology obsolescence and physical deterioration."[4]

The challenges in maintaining access to digital resources over time are related to notable differences between digital and paper-based material:

- Machine Dependency. Digital materials all require specific hardware and software in order to access them.
- The speed of changes in technology means that the timeframe during which action must be taken is very much shorter than for paper. Timeframes during which action needs to be taken is measured in a few years, perhaps only 2-5, as opposed to decades or even centuries we associate with the preservation of traditional materials. Technology obsolescence is generally regarded as the greatest technical threat to ensuring continued access to digital material.
- Fragility of the media. The media digital materials are stored on is inherently unstable and without suitable storage conditions and management can deteriorate very quickly even though it may not appear to be damaged externally.
- The ease with which changes can be made and the need to make some changes in order to manage the material means that there are challenges associated with ensuring the continued integrity, authenticity, and history of digital materials.
- The implications of allocating priorities are much more severe than for paper. A digital resource which is not selected for active preservation treatment at an early stage will very likely be lost or unusable in the near future.
- The nature of the technology requires a life-cycle management approach to be taken to its maintenance. A continual programme of active management is needed from the design and creation stage if preservation is to be successful. This in turn leads to much more involvement both within and between institutions and changing roles.

The above issues are all interconnected and mean that a radically different approach is required in managing digital materials than for paper-based materials, one in which action needs to be taken, and planned for, at regular intervals. Retrospective preservation of digital materials is at best costly, possibly prohibitively so for any but the most highly valued, and at worst impossible. While concrete cost examples are few, it is widely acknowledged that the most cost-effective means of ensuring continued access to important digital materials is to consider the preservation implications as early as possible, preferably at creation, and actively to plan for their management throughout their lifecycle.

What digital materials are being produced?

Digital materials range from relatively simple, text-based files (e.g. word processing files), to highly sophisticated web-based resources which fully exploit the benefits of the technology (e.g. combining sound with images, the ability to link to other resources, the ability to interrogate the data). There have been numerous projects to digitise collections of texts and images, primarily to utilise digital technology to improve access to these materials, which would otherwise require a visit to the holding institution.

Increasingly, resources are being created for which there is no analogue equivalent. These "born digital" materials utilise the technology to provide a level of convenience and functionality which is not possible in the analogue environment. For example, dynamic databases which are constantly updated, to produce large scale mapping or on demand publications, are continuing to proliferate. These utilise the technology very effectively for current access but pose considerable challenges in terms of the ability to maintain access to them over time and also the ability to compare data at different points in time.

Both digital surrogates of analogue originals and "born digital" resources will ultimately pose similar challenges in terms of ensuring their continued survival, though the latter may be considered the most vulnerable as there is no analogue original if they are lost[5]. In general, the more complex the materials, the more challenging it will be to ensure that they remain accessible and retain the same functionality over time.

Who needs to be involved?

Because of the nature of digital materials, as outlined above, the ability to preserve access to them well into the future depends upon the involvement of a wide range of stakeholders. Principal among these are the creators of digital content, whose involvement in their preservation might involve, for example, consideration of standards in terms of format and media, and ensuring enough documentation is available to enable their management by others. Another key stakeholder will be institutions which act as long-term repositories for digital materials. They must establish an ongoing dialogue with creators and a pro-active approach to potential future accessions.

The nature of digital technology dictates that it is not feasible simply to hand over stewardship of the resource at some point in the future, without having managed it sufficiently to facilitate management by whatever repository has accepted long-term preservation responsibility. Large institutions involved in creating digital materials may most sensibly be the ones which retain them over time, thus ensuring maximum return on the initial investment of creation. Co-operative models for long-term preservation might include a number of organisations, some of which may have experience in ensuring the preservation of paper-based materials and seek logically to extend this remit to their digital counterparts, while others may specialise in particular subject areas and/or particular types of digital materials.

All public institutions such as archives, libraries, and museums need to be involved in applying their professional skills and expertise to the long-term preservation of digital materials, just as they have taken a role in the preservation of traditional materials. Throughout the world, some of these institutions have taken a strong leadership role in addressing the practical implications of digital preservation.

For some organisations, it may prove more cost-effective to contract all or part of their digital preservation responsibilities to a third party. Nevertheless, staff will need to be sufficiently aware of digital preservation issues, particularly as they relate to legal, organisational and contractual problems, to manage these third party contracts effectively.

Whatever model is adopted for the long term, it will need to involve the co-operation and participation of all who have an interest in creating, acquiring and making accessible, digital materials.

How much does it cost?

Digital preservation is essentially about preserving access over time. This makes it virtually impossible neatly to segregate costs which are only for digital preservation from costs which are only about access. Access costs are significant because both the technology and user expectations advance at a very rapid rate. The initial technical infrastructure costs required for creating and/or acquiring digital materials and providing access to them are substantial. It makes sense to consider means of protecting this investment from the outset though this has rarely been a consideration to date.

The assumption that preservation costs will be greater in the digital environment than for paper is based on four interrelated factors:

- The need actively to manage inevitable changes in technology at regular intervals and over a (potentially) infinite timeframe.
- The lack of standardisation in both the resources themselves and the licensing agreements with publishers and other data producers, making economies of scale difficult to achieve.
- The as yet unresolved means of reliably and accurately rendering certain digital publications so that they do not lose essential information after technology changes.
- That for some time to come digital preservation may be an additional cost on top of the costs for traditional collections unless cost savings can be realised. Institutions with responsibility for both digital and traditional collections, such

as deposit libraries, face the most difficult challenge, as they need to balance resources equitably between two quite different requirements. These institutions are also more likely to have a higher priority on long-term preservation as opposed to short-term access. There is scope for shared cost models and these may prove to be the most cost-effective in the long term.

While there is understandable concern that the costs of preserving digital materials will be high, it is equally important to consider the costs and implications of not preserving them. The costs of recreating a digital resource may be much higher than that for preserving it; further, the opportunity to do so may no longer exist[6]. An increasing dependence on both digitally produced and accessed information means that there is a rapidly growing body of digital material for which there are legal, ethical, economic and/or cultural imperatives to retain, at least for a defined period of time and, in some cases, forever. If active steps are not taken to protect these digital materials, they will inevitably become inaccessible within a relatively brief timeframe.

References to sources of information for various categories of costs, from digitisation to calculating the costs of preserving digital objects over time can be found in the Further Reading section of **4.1.**

The issue of cost is also discussed in **2.2.2**, where it is intended to be used as a basis for awareness raising and improved understanding of cost elements as they relate to organisations.

References

1. See for example the Catriona II project, which discovered that quality resources were being created in Scottish Universities, 'However, since they are not being created with the aim of wider access and use, they are mostly not networked, difficult to find, or in difficult to access formats'. These findings might reasonably be expected to be extrapolated to other UK institutions and by no means confined to the higher education sector. <http://wp269.lib.strath.ac.uk5050/Cat2/index.html

2. Waters, D and Garrett, J. (1996). Preserving Digital Information: Report of the Task Force on Archiving of Digital Information commissioned by the Commission on Preservation and Access and the Research Libraries Group. Washington, DC: Commission on Preservation and Access. Also available online at:
<http://www.rlg.org/ArchTF> or <http://www.rlg.ac.uk/ArchTF>

3. Long Term Preservation of Electronic Materials (1995). A Report of a Workshop Organised by JISC/British Library, held at the University of Warwick on 27-28 November 1995. British Library R & D Report 6238. <http://www.ukoln.ac.uk/services/papers/bl/rdr6238>

4. Hedstrom, M. and Montgomery, S. (1998). Digital Preservation Needs and Requirements in RLG Member Institutions. Mountain View CA: RLG. p. 3. <http://www.rlg.ac.uk/preserv/digpres.html>

5. For example, the PRO's strategy states that preservation systems must be capable of providing a guarantee of rates of data loss no greater than 1 in 100,000 for data surrogates and 1 in 100,000,000 for "born digital" objects where no originals exist from which to re-create the object. Source: A Digital Preservation Strategy for the PRO. 1999. 3.6.3.

6. For example it has been reported that it costs about $5-7 per megabyte per year to retain electronic engineering records in the US but about $1250 per megabyte to re-create them. See <http://ssdoo.gsfc.nasa.gov/nost/isoas/us01/minutes.html>.
Costs involved in creating other digital resources, e.g. satellite or archaeological data may be higher. In addition, the data may be unique and unrecoverable if destroyed.

2.2 Preservation Issues

2.2.1 Technological Issues

Digital media

"Digital materials are especially vulnerable to loss and destruction because they are stored on fragile magnetic and optical media that deteriorate rapidly and that can fail suddenly from exposure to heat, humidity, airborne contaminants, or faulty reading and writing devices."[1]

Digital media are subject to destruction and deterioration in new ways, though unintended loss can be avoided if procedures are adapted to the needs of the technology. Precautions can be taken which will help significantly to reduce the danger of loss and include:

* Storing in a stable, controlled environment.
* Implementing regular refreshment cycles to copy onto newer media.
* Making preservation copies (assuming licensing/copyright permission).
* Implementing appropriate handling procedures.
* Transferring to "standard" storage media.

However, while the media on which the information are stored may or may not fail, what is certain is that technology will change rapidly so that even if the media is retained in pristine condition, it may still not be possible to access the information it contains. No matter how exemplary the care of the media is, it will not remove the requirement to deal with changes in technology, though responsible care should make it easier to manage technology changes.

Changes in technology

"Unlike the situation that applies to books, digital archiving requires relatively frequent investments to overcome rapid obsolescence introduced by galloping technological change."[2]

Because digital material is machine dependent, it is not possible to access the information unless there is appropriate hardware, and associated software which will make it intelligible. Technology advances even in the past decade illustrate this point:

* $5\frac{1}{4}$ inch floppy disks have been superseded by $3\frac{1}{2}$ inch floppy disks;

* There have been several upgrades to Windows software since it was first introduced and it would now be very difficult to convert from earlier versions to the current versions;

* Thousands of software programs common in the early 1990s are now extinct and unavailable.

The certainty that there will be frequent technological change poses a major challenge and it is therefore not surprising that collection managers quoted in the RLG survey cited technological obsolescence as the greatest threat to successful digital preservation. Precautions can, and should be taken, which will greatly reduce the risk of inadvertently losing access to a resource because of changes in technology. These include:

- Using standard file and media formats, as recommended by reputable sources.

- Providing detailed documentation to enable both context to be determined and also to facilitate successful management. (Guides to good practice are available, some of these are provided in **4.4**.).

Authenticity and context

"At each stage of the cycle, electronic records need to be actively managed according to established procedures, to ensure that they retain qualities of integrity, authenticity and reliability."[3]

While it is technically feasible to alter records in a paper environment, the relative ease with which this can be achieved in the digital environment, either deliberately or inadvertently, has given this issue more pressing urgency. The Public Record Office (PRO) mandates mechanisms in accordance with BSI/PD0008 for its own records[4]. The PRO draft strategy suggests that the best way to achieve authenticity is through a combination of proper processes (as outlined in their guidance documents) with data integrity mechanisms such as MD5 signatures generated at the time of ingest and the establishment of audit trails for all actions. Duranti [5] makes a useful distinction between authentication (the means used to prove that a record is what it purports to be at a given time) and authenticity (a concept already familiar in archival science and which refers to the quality of the record itself and its essential contextual information). Records management systems need to be able to link to essential contextual information regarding the business procedures of the creating agency. Authenticity and integrity of digital resources can be equally important in other sectors. For example, scholars will need to feel confident that references they cite will stay the same over time, courts of law will need to be assured that material can withstand legal evidential requirements, government departments may well have legally enforceable requirements regarding authenticity, and so on. This issue overlaps with both legal and organisational issues and it may be one which is best resolved within individual sectors rather than through generic procedures.

Scale

Although computer storage is increasing in scale and its relative cost is decreasing constantly, the quantity of data and our ability to capture it with relative ease still matches or exceeds it in a number of areas. Some repositories still face significant challenges in developing and maintaining scaleable architectures and procedures to handle huge quantities of data generated from sources such as satellites or the web. The technical and managerial challenges in accessioning, managing and providing access to digital materials on this scale should not be underestimated.

Strategies

"Three…approaches to digital preservation have been developed:
- Preserve the original software (and possible hardware) that was used to create and access the information. This is known as the technology preservation strategy. It also involves preserving both the original operating system and hardware on which to run it.
- Program future powerful computer systems to emulate older, obsolete computer platforms and operating systems as required. This is the technology emulation strategy.
- Ensure that the digital information is re-encoded in new formats before the old format becomes obsolete. This is the digital information migration strategy." [6]

Strategies for some formats are well established and tested over time. For example, migration has been used for electronic text, image, and database applications by the computing industry and a number of data archives and centres for decades.

However, all three of the current strategies have potential drawbacks in some circumstances.

The need for further research has been recognised and appropriate strategies are being tested but technology will continue to evolve and will continue to raise new issues. It may well be that there will never be a single definitive strategy and a range of strategies appropriate to different categories of digital materials may need to be employed. In this way a parallel can be drawn with the paper environment which also utilises a range of preservation strategies (de-acidification, microfilming, appropriate storage and handling etc.). The major difference, and the major cause of concern in the digital environment, is that failure to address the long-term access requirements of digital materials at a very much earlier stage than for paper materials will almost inevitably result in their permanent loss.

See **4.3** for more detailed discussion of digital preservation strategies.

2.2.2 Organisational Issues

While technological issues are undeniably challenging, there are also numerous challenges which relate to the ability of organisations to integrate the management of digital materials into their organisational structure. In addition, there is an increasing need to go beyond the confines of individual organisations, or even countries, to maximise the benefits of the technology, address issues such as copyright, and also to overcome the challenges cost-effectively. Most organisations readily acknowledge the benefits of increased collaboration but also indicate the difficulties of, what one case study interviewee described as "differing agendas and timescales", not to mention different funding mechanisms. The following issues are being faced, and in many cases, systematically addressed, by organisations world-wide.

Costs

"Part of the difficulty in understanding costs has been the lack of working examples from which to learn and the difficulty in extrapolating costs from pilot projects (of which there have been many) to full-scale public services." [7]

As the above quote illustrates, there is a wide and potentially misleading amount of project-related data on costs which may or may not have any bearing on the costs of managing digital materials long-term. It is important to differentiate costs for digitisation, for which there are more reliable cost models (though still needing to be interpreted with care), from the costs of managing digital materials, whether those materials are produced as a result of digitising analogue materials or whether they are "born digital". This manual is primarily concerned with the costs of preserving access to important digital materials over time, however those materials were created. In that context, the costs of creating digital materials are relevant in so far as they need to include cost elements which will ultimately facilitate their long-term preservation.

The difficulties in isolating costs for preservation from access costs is referred to in **2.1**. Beagrie and Greenstein[8] identified seven areas of concern needing to be addressed by organisations, only one of which is preservation but all of which significantly overlap. Hendley[9] also referred to the difficulties this imposes on developing meaningful and reliable cost models. In predicting likely costs, organisations will need to consider both the quantity and level of access they intend to provide as these factors will be significant influences on costs.

As indicated in Organisational Issues: Expertise (page 28), the ability to employ and develop staff with appropriate skills is made more difficult by the speed of technological change and the range of skills needed. It is also limited by resource constraints on organisations which may well need to retain the same level of ongoing commitment to and management of traditional collections and may need to integrate commitment to digital collections without additional resources.

Because costs for both technical and organisational infrastructure are still not well defined organisations are confronted with the requirement to commit to the principle to safeguard significant digital assets, without a clear idea of the associated costs over time. This makes forward planning a somewhat more hazardous activity and one in which organisations need to begin to take action but may be unwilling to do so without more concrete assurances of costs. This requires faith that cost-effective solutions are more likely to emerge once organisations have sufficient practical experience in managing digital collections. This experience is also likely greatly to improve the prospects for effective collaboration, which is based on a shared understanding of the practicalities involved. An approach which builds incrementally on practice within the institution and collaboration with others who are confronting the same challenges will reduce risk and help develop effective strategies and practices.

(See also **3.1** for further discussion on the advantages of co-operation between creating and archiving organisations to reduce costs. See also **4.1** for references to models for specific aspects of costs, such as digitisation, and maintaining digital archives.)

Expertise
"The need for digital preservation expertise is high: asked to rate staff as expert, intermediate, or novice, only 8 of the 54 institutions considered their staff at the expert level."[10]

The dramatic speed of technological change means that few organisations have been able even fully to articulate what their needs are in this area, much less employ or develop staff with appropriate skills. In addition, there is little in the way of appropriate training and "learning by doing" can often be the most practical interim measure. The DLM Forum[11] has been undertaking work in this area for records management and has made significant progress in terms of identifying a set of six core competencies which have been used as the basis for developing training programmes for records managers.

It will take time for these developments to filter through to the workplace, and in the meantime, organisations and professional organisations need to ensure their existing staff and members can develop, and continue to develop, the range of competencies they need to manage the digital materials in their care. In addition, continuous professional development will be at least as necessary for dealing with digital materials as it is for other developmental needs. Case study interviewers have stressed the need for focussed, tailor-made courses to provide them with their specific requirements. This handbook aims to help fill a gap between current needs and existing training courses by providing guidance and tools which can be used by individuals, institutions and trainers to meet current needs.

Organisational structures

"In addition to redefining responsibilities of organisations, it may be necessary to redefine roles within organisations to ensure long-term access to digital information."[12]

The nature of the technology and dependencies in the preservation of digital materials are such that there are implications for organisational structures. Organisational structures tend to be segregated into discrete elements for the efficient processing of traditional collections, but will need to cross boundaries in order to draw on the full range of skills and expertise required for digital materials. Many of the activities converge, for example decisions about acquisition and preservation should sensibly be made at the same time. Even with clearly articulated policies in place, this is likely to place strains on resources which may be seen to be competing, at least in the interim. In the absence of strong policy development, it will be impossible to develop effective strategies for managing digital materials. In a worst case scenario, it may even result in a situation in which the management of both traditional and digital materials is placed at risk.

Roles

"Although there is continuity of purpose and value within cultural institutions, these exist alongside a fundamental examination of roles and practices."[13]

There are some existing repositories which undertake responsibility for specific subject areas or specific formats. In the UK, for example, the Arts and Humanities Data Service and Data Archive are two examples of institutions undertaking responsibility for social science and humanities research data, while the National Sound Archive assumes responsibility for its collection of sound recordings. In addition, there is work going on in other countries to establish national co-operative models for digital preservation. Examples of these can be found in **3.1**. In time, it is expected that these efforts in individual countries will crystallise into clearly defined roles and responsibilities where it is as obvious which institution is likely to be the major preserver of specific digital materials as it is for non digital materials. Despite these encouraging developments, at the present time the question of who should be responsible for ensuring long-term preservation is by no means as established in the digital environment as it is in the analogue environment.

Even when it has been determined which organisations will undertake to act on their long-term digital preservation responsibilities the environment will demand far greater engagement with a much larger group of stakeholders than has previously been the case. Some will inevitably choose to contract out all or part of their digital preservation responsibilities to a third party provider. The lifecycle approach advocated by Beagrie and Greenstein[8] has significant implications for the way organisations responsible for long-term preservation need to interact and collaborate with data producers and publishers and each other.

Roles are also changing within as well as between institutions. Assigning responsibility for preservation of digital materials acquired and/or created by an organisation will inevitably require involvement with personnel from different parts of the organisation working together. This can potentially present difficulties unless underpinned by a strong corporate vision which can be communicated to staff. Similarly, staff working in an increasingly electronic environment are needing to modify their role to reflect the different demands of the technology.

Finally, creators of digital materials need to be able to understand the implications of their actions in terms of the medium to long-term viability of the digital material they create. Whether it be a record created during the day-to-day business of the department, a digital copy of analogue collection material, or a "born digital" resource, guidance and support as well as an appropriate technical and organisational infrastructure will assist in facilitating greatly improved prospects for efficient management and preservation.

Selection

"In the network environment, any individual with access to the Internet can be a publisher and the network publishing process does not always provide the initial screening and selection at the manuscript stage on which libraries have traditionally relied in the print environment."[14]

The enormous quantity of information being produced digitally, its variable quality, and the resource constraints on those taking responsibility to preserve long-term access, makes selectivity inevitable if the objective is to preserve ongoing access. In the digital environment, it is possible to by-pass the traditional distribution channels, as well as filtering and quality control processes. While there are benefits for users in terms of swift access, there are also difficulties in terms of quality control. Selecting quality materials for long-term retention therefore places a burden on organisations in terms of resources and also in terms of the potential impact of selection.

With traditional collections, lack of selection for preservation may not necessarily mean that the item will be lost, allowing for a comfort zone of potential changes in criteria for selection at a later stage. No such comfort zone exists in the digital environment where non-selection for preservation will almost certainly mean loss of the item, even if it is subsequently considered to be worthwhile.

In cases where there may be multiple versions, decisions must be made in selecting which version is the best one for preservation, or whether more than one should be selected. Sampling dynamic resources as opposed to attempting to save each change, may be the only practical option but may have severe repercussions if the sampling is not undertaken within a well-defined framework and with due regard to the anticipated contemporary and future needs of the users.

Some consideration also needs to be given in the selection to the level of redundancy needed to ensure digital preservation. A level of redundancy with multiple copies held in different repositories is inherent in traditional print materials and has contributed to their preservation over centuries. Although in a digital environment a single institution can provide world-wide access and accept preservation responsibility, it remains an issue of concern to many that a level of redundancy should exist in the digital environment. Such concerns need to be balanced against the potential cost in duplication of effort. Either scenario points to a greater level of overt collaboration in selection between institutions to preserve electronic publications. In any scenario, it will be critical to establish sustainability and unequivocal acceptance of responsibility to avoid the danger of losing access over time. There still needs to be assurance that preservation responsibility will be undertaken, and a clear understanding of who will undertake that responsibility and for what period of time. Otherwise there can be no guarantee that, even if several copies are stored in various repositories, all of those repositories might, for a variety of reasons, cease maintenance of the digital object at some point.

Finally, in all successful preservation strategies it may well be necessary to repeat steps in the selection process, with appropriate documentation, as part of the long-term cycle of actions to maintain access in new technological environments.

See also **4.2.1**.

2.2.3 Legal Issues

"Compounding the technical challenges of migrating digital information is the problem of managing the process in a legal and organizational environment that is in flux as it moves to accommodate rapidly changing digital technologies."[15]

This section provides an overview of legal issues involved in digital preservation. As such it does not attempt to provide guidance on general legal issues which impact on the operations of libraries, archives and other repositories, as these are covered in a number of other reference works. It is written from a UK perspective and legislation in this area will vary from country to country. It is also an area even in the UK where forthcoming legislation such as the draft EU Copyright Directive may have a substantial future impact. Please note this section does not constitute legal advice. This is a complex and rapidly changing area and readers must seek legal advice for their specific circumstances and national legal frameworks. Further information on implementation and further reading is listed in **3.4**.

Intellectual property rights (IPR) and preservation:
Copyright and other intellectual property rights (IPR) such as moral rights have a substantial impact on digital preservation. As outlined in **2.2.1** the preservation of digital materials is dependent on a range of strategies, which has implications for IPR in those materials. The IPR issues in digital materials are arguably more complex and significant than for traditional media and if not addressed can impede or even prevent preservation activities. Consideration may need to be given not only to content but to any associated software. Simply copying (refreshing) digital materials onto another medium, encapsulating content and software for emulation, or migrating content to new hardware and software, all involve activities which can infringe IPR unless statutory exemptions exist or specific permissions have been obtained from rights holders.

As both migration and emulation will involve manipulation and changing presentation and functionality to some degree (especially over any period of time) important issues of principle and practice are raised in negotiations. It is important to establish a dialogue with rights holders so that they are fully aware of these issues and the actions and rights required to ensure the preservation of selected items.

What is different about IPR and electronic materials?
Traditional materials are relatively stable and well established legal and organisational frameworks for preservation are in place. This is not the case for electronic materials. Digital materials need consideration of both content and also hardware and software, and require very different methods of preservation. In addition in the UK there are currently no similar legal

provisions for prescribed libraries and archives permitting preservation activities on electronic items in their permanent collections: the necessary permissions must be obtained from copyright holders.

The duration of IPR in electronic materials will often extend well beyond commercial interests in them and the technology which was used to generate them. Long-term preservation and access may require migration of the material into new forms or emulation of the original operating environment: all of which may be impossible without appropriate legal permissions from the original rights owners of the content and underlying software.

Legal deposit of electronic publications

The position on legal deposit of electronic publications in the UK is different from that of print publications (the current Act refers only and specifically to print). Voluntary deposit arrangements were introduced in January 2000. Statutory provision for legal deposit of electronic publications may follow within two years. However, voluntary arrangements need to be negotiated on a case by case basis.

Other statutory requirements

Other statutory requirements may also apply and influence preservation of digital resources. The requirements of the Public Records Act will apply to government records including those in electronic form. Statutory retention periods will apply to many electronic records (e.g. for accounting and tax purposes). Although these are often of limited duration, it is notable that requirements for retention of electronic records in some sectors (e.g. the pharmaceutical industry), are of increasingly long duration. In such cases long-term preservation strategies will apply as technological change will almost certainly have affected access to such records.

Access and security

Some of the additional complexity in IPR issues relates to the fact that electronic materials are also easily copied and re-distributed. Rights holders are therefore particularly concerned with controlling access and potential infringements of copyright. Technology developed to address these concerns and provide copyright protection measures can also inhibit or prevent actions needed for preservation. These concerns over access and infringement and preservation need to be understood by organisations preserving digital materials and addressed by both parties in negotiating rights and procedures for preservation.

Business models and licensing

Consideration of the business models for dissemination of electronic materials and the range of stakeholders also impacts on IPR and preservation. In most cases electronic publications (particularly electronic journals) are not physically owned by the subscribers, who license access from the publisher. Subscribers are therefore concerned that publishers consider the archiving and preservation of these works and include archiving and perpetual access to back issues in licensing of these works.

Stakeholders, contract and grant conditions, and moral rights

Electronic materials are the result of substantial financial investment by public funds (e.g. research councils) and/or publishers and intellectual investment by individual scholars and authors. Each of these stakeholders may have an interest in preservation; the archiving organisation will need to acquire permissions from them to safeguard and maximise the financial investment or the intellectual and cultural value of the work for future generations. Such interests may be manifested through contract, licence, and grant conditions or through statutory provision such as "moral rights" for the authors.

Privacy and confidentiality

Information held within the repository may be subject to the Data Protection Act or similar privacy legislation protecting information held on individuals. Information may also be subject to confidentiality agreements. Privacy and confidentiality concerns may impact on how digital materials can be managed within the repository or by third parties, and made accessible for use.

Investment in deposited materials by the repository

Holders of the material over many decades will almost certainly need to invest resources to generate revised documentation and metadata and generate new forms of the material if access is to be maintained. Additional IPR issues in this new investment needs to be anticipated and future re-use of such materials considered.

Where a depositor or licensor retains the right to withdraw materials from the archive and significant investment could be anticipated in these materials over time by the holding institution, withdrawal fees to compensate for any investment may be built into deposit agreements.

References

1. Hedstrom, M. and Montgomery, S. (1998). Digital Preservation Needs and Requirements in RLG Member Institutions. Mountain View CA: RLG. p. 1. Also available online at: <http://www.rlg.ac.uk/preserv/digpres.html>

2. Feeney, M. (ed). (1999). Digital Culture: Maximising the Nation's Investment. London: The National Preservation Office. p.11. Also available online at: <http://www.ukoln.ac.uk/services/elib/papers/other/jisc-npo-dig/intro.html>

3. Public Record Office. (1999). Guidelines on the Management, Appraisal and Preservation of Electronic Records. Kew: Public Record Office. Volume 1: Principles. 4.4. Available free from the PRO or online at: <http://www.pro.gov.uk/recordsmanagement/eros/guidelines>

4. British Standards Institution (1999). Code of Practice for Legal Admissibility and Evidential Weight of Information Stored Electronically. DISC PD 0008:1999.

5. Duranti, L. (2000). The Impact of Technological Changes on Archival Theory. International Congress of Archives, Seville, September 2000. <http://www.interpares.org/documents/ld_sevilla_2000.pdf>

6. Feeney (1999). op.cit. p.41.

7. Ashley, K. (1999). Digital Archive Costs: Facts and Fallacies. DLM Forum '99. p. 1. <http://europa.eu.int/ISPO/dlm/fulltext/full_ash_en.htm>

8. Beagrie, N and Greenstein, D. (1998). A Strategic Policy Framework for Creating and Preserving Digital Collections. British Library Research and Innovation Report 107. London: The British Library. Also available online at: <http://ahds.ac.uk/strategic.htm>

9. Hendley, T. (1998). Comparison of Methods and Costs of Digital Preservation. British Library Research and Innovation Report 67. London: The British Library. Also available online at: <http://www.ukoln.ac.uk/services/elib/papers/tavistock/hendley/hendley.html>

10. Hedstrom, M. and Montgomery, S. (1998) op.cit. p.41.

11. A European forum for archivists and records managers. Its stated aim is "to achieve multidisciplinary Europe-wide co-operation to produce guidelines and to provide support to solving the issues dealing with electronic records." <http://europa.eu.int/ISPO/dlm>

12. PADI website. Issues: Roles and Responsibilities. Roles within organisations. <http://www.nla.gov.au/padi/topics/8.html>

13. Dempsey, L. (1999). Scientific, Industrial, and Cultural Heritage: a shared approach. Ariadne (22). December 1999. p. 4.
<http://www.ariadne.ac.uk/issue22/dempsey>

14. National Library of Canada. (1998). Networked Electronic Publications: Policy and Guidelines. p.3.
<http://www.nlc-bnc.ca/9/8/index-e.html>

15. Waters, D and Garrett, J. (1996). Preserving Digital Information: Report of the Task Force on Archiving of Digital Information commissioned by the Commission on Preservation and Access and the Research Libraries Group. Washington, DC: Commission on Preservation and Access. p.13. Also available online at:
<http://www.rlg.ac.uk/ArchTF> or <http://www.rlg.ac.uk/ArchTF>

3.   Institutional Strategies

Intended primary audience

Both senior administrators and operational managers within institutions.
Also existing or potential third-party service providers.

Assumed level of knowledge of digital preservation

Intermediate (basic understanding of the issues, some practical experience).

Purpose

- To form the basis for further development of policies and strategies
  appropriate to individual institutions.
- To provide existing examples of good practice which might serve as models.

This chapter outlines a number of strategies which have been used
successfully by institutions in developing approaches to digital preservation.
Each section discusses the approach, its potential advantages and
disadvantages, and then provides exemplars of the approach together with
further reading on the topic. Strategies such as these will form a core
component of corporate policy development to address digital preservation.
Sound policy development combined with effective working practices and
procedures (see **chapter 4**) has been essential to effective digital
preservation programmes.

3.1 Collaboration

There are compelling reasons and, in some cases, political pressure, to engage in greater collaboration within and between organisations in order effectively to confront and overcome the challenges of digital preservation. The range of skills required to do this demands flexibility within organisational structures to facilitate working in multi-disciplinary teams. There is a significant overlap in the digital preservation issues being faced by all organisations and across all sectors so it makes sense to capitalise on the potential benefits of pooling expertise and experience.

Internal collaboration

The usual assumption is that collaboration is external. However, most libraries and archives are managing a combination of paper-based and digital resources for the foreseeable future and will need to structure their organisation to manage the disparate needs of the two. The blurring of boundaries which digital technology produces means that sections and departments which are structurally distinct, will now need to co-operate in order to integrate the preservation and management of digital materials with other materials.

Such co-operation may well prove impossible unless there are mechanisms put in place to facilitate it. At the strategic level, a cross disciplinary committee charged with developing and overseeing objectives is one means of ensuring that the involvement of all relevant sections can be brought together[1]. At the operational level, consideration will need to be given to defining what specific tasks are required and where those responsibilities logically lie. Setting up of working groups to investigate specific issues is one means of blending the range of skills required[2].

Advantages
* Makes good use of available skills and expertise.
* Promotes team working.
* Recognises the diversity of skills required for the digital environment in general and digital preservation in particular.
* Is much more likely to yield a good outcome in the longer term.

Disadvantages
* May be frustrating and time consuming in the short term.
* Communication may be difficult initially.
* Senior management may be unwilling to risk perceived lack of control.
* Staff may feel uncomfortable with new ways of working.
* Organisational structures may not be sufficiently flexible to facilitate effective collaboration between different sections.
See also **3.5**.

External collaboration

External collaboration can include formal agreements between two or more organisations and informal arrangements between colleagues working in different institutions and possibly also across different sectors. See also **3.2**.

Formal agreements can range from collaborative agreements for simply sharing information to accomplishing a specific task (for example working groups), or agreeing on specific allocation of archiving responsibilities. Clearly, the more complex the nature of the agreement, and the more differences there are between participating organisations in terms of their business needs, the more difficult it is likely to be to achieve, though the longer term benefits may also be greater.

Advantages

- Organisational commitment and authority.
- Clear allocation of responsibility.
- Clearly identified gains.
- Enhanced understanding of complex issues.
- Economies of scale – the sum being greater than the parts.
- Greater practical benefit from pooled resources and expertise.
- Greater political and economic clout.
- Improved prospects for future mutually beneficial collaboration.

Disadvantages

- Difficulty of establishing unambiguous agreements able to be accepted by all parties.
- Time taken to establish them.
- Difficulties of communicating across different professional and organisational frameworks.
- Potential bureaucratic barriers.

Informal arrangements have always played an important role in maintaining current awareness among colleagues in similar disciplines. Digital technology provides an increased imperative to share experience and information in an emerging discipline as well as a simpler and more rapid means to contact colleagues known to be working in areas of interest.

Advantages

- Specific to individuals and their personal development and interest.
- Speed and ease of communication.
- Efficient transfer of information.

Disadvantages

- Potential to side-step wider organisational perspective.
- May miss the potential for wider dissemination of knowledge unless there are organisational mechanisms in place to facilitate sharing of knowledge.

References

1. DLM Forum. (1997). Guidelines on the Best Practices for Using Electronic Information. p. 20 regards the setting up of a multidisciplinary team to define and monitor a global strategy as best practice. <http://europa.eu.int/ISPO/dlm/documents/gdlines.pdf>

2. Lee, S. (1999). Scoping the Future of the University of Oxford's Digital Library Collections: Final Report. p.30. Recommends establishing working parties on metadata and delivery systems. <http://www.bodley.ox.ac.uk/scoping/report.html>

Exemplars and Further Reading

1. AHDS (Arts and Humanities Data Service)
    <http://ahds.ac.uk>

    The AHDS is a distributed service consisting of five service providers
    (Archaeology Data Service; History Data Service; Oxford Text Archive;
    Performing Arts Data Service; Visual Arts Data Service) and the Executive.
    The aim of the AHDS is to collect, preserve, and promote re-use of the
    electronic resources resulting from arts and humanities research.

2. Cedars (CURL Exemplars in Digital Archives)
    <http://www.leeds.ac.uk/cedars>

    A three-year eLib project which commenced in 1998 and is led by the
    universities of Oxford, Cambridge, and Leeds on behalf of CURL. The UK
    Office for Library and Information Networking (UKOLN) is also a partner,
    with particular emphasis on the development of preservation metadata. The
    main goal of the project is "to address strategic, methodological and practical
    issues and provide guidance in best practice for digital preservation".

3. Digital Library Federation. Preservation of electronic scholarly journals.
    <http://www.clir.org/diglib/preserve/presjour.htm>

    An initiative commenced by the Coalition for Networked Information (CNI) and
    the Council on Library and Information Resources (CLIR). The objectives are to
    establish archival repositories; seek publishing partners to populate the archives;
    develop the necessary licensing apparatus to ensure libraries' interests are
    accommodated by archiving strategies being adopted by the repositories; and
    share experience of publishers, libraries, and repositories to mutual advantage.
    The initiative has also defined minimum criteria for a digital archive repository
    which is based on the OAIS model but has been recast to reflect the specific
    needs of libraries and publishers. A draft document has also been prepared
    which encourages merging digital archives and repositories to document and
    enclose their practices in particular areas. This is further indication of the
    progress towards defining operational requirements and preservation
    responsibilities based on practical experience.

4. National Digital Preservation Coalition

    In 2000 the JISC under the aegis of its Committee for Electronic Information
    (JCEI) created a new post, the Digital Preservation Focus, in recognition of the
    increasing strategic importance of digital preservation for the Higher and Further
    Education communities. A key task will be the establishment of a National Digital
    Preservation Coalition in the UK. Details of this will be available from the JISC
    Digital Preservation Focus site when established. In the interim, further information
    may be found at the JISC website available at: <http://www.jisc.ac.uk>

5. National Library of Canada. Consultation on Online Publications
<http://www.nlc-bnc.ca/bulletin/2000/jun2000e/01e.htm>

An initiative of the National Library of Canada aimed at bringing together key experts from various sectors of the Canadian publishing community with NLC staff to discuss Canadian online publishing issues. This is another example of the leadership role being taken by national libraries to confront the issues associated with electronic publishing and develop strategies to deal with them. While this initiative is seen as preliminary, the NLC "considers it to be the start of a process towards a strategy that meets common objectives".

6. NEDLIB (Networked European Deposit Library)
<http://www.konbib.nl/nedlib>

This project has twelve partners consisting of deposit libraries, archives, and IT developers. Three publishers are also contributing to the project, which runs from January 1998 to December 2000. As well as collaboration between the partners, the NEDLIB website and discussion list, NEDLIB-INT actively encourages communication with others working on the same things.

The three aims of NEDLIB are:
1. To develop a common architectural framework and basic tools for building deposit systems for electronic publications;
2. To address the issue of long-term preservation;
3. To build a demonstrator system, with tools and software, covering all functional aspects of a deposit system for electronic publications (DSEP).

7. PANDORA (Preserving and Accessing Networked Documentary Resources of Australia)
<http://pandora.nla.gov.au>

The PANDORA project began as a National Library of Australia initiative. Once the proof-of-concept archive was established, the NLA sought other deposit libraries as partners to join them in preserving Australian online documentary heritage. This involves state libraries, the other deposit institutions which, with the NLA, have a mandate to collect and preserve Australian non-digital documentary heritage.

8. RLG-DLF 1999 Task Force on Policy and Practice for Long-Term Retention of Digital Materials.
<http://www.rlg.ac.uk/preserv/digrlgdlf99.html>

An example of collaboration between two membership organisations, Research Libraries Group (RLG) and Digital Library Federation (DLF) which have both made digital preservation a key priority for action and attention. This Task Force was formed in response to a 1998 survey of digital preservation needs and requirements in RLG member institutions.

9. RLG/OCLC
<http://www.rlg.ac.uk/pr/pr2000-oclc.html>

Once again RLG is in partnership with another organisation, in this case, Online Computer Library Center (OCLC). RLG and OCLC are two organisations that have done much separately to progress digital preservation issues but now feel it is timely to explore how they can co-operate to create infrastructures for digital archiving. The first steps towards this wider aim are collaboration on two working documents, one on characteristics of reliable archiving services and another on preservation metadata.

10. Reference Model for an Open Archival Information System (OAIS) Draft Recommendation for Space Data System Standard. May 1999.
<http://www.ccsds.org/RP9905/RP9905.html>

The Consultative Committee for Space Data Systems (CCSDS) has been asked by the International Standards Organisation (ISO) to co-ordinate the development of standards to support the long-term preservation of digital information obtained from observations of the terrestrial and space environments. The OAIS Reference Model is the first of this co-ordination effort to reach draft standard and is being used, or at least adapted by an increasing number of organisations. Though initially intended for a fairly specific application, it is intended to be used in a wide range of archiving organisations. This is a good example of both the advantages (consensus; increased consistency; utilising wide ranging expertise and experience) and disadvantages (time to reach widespread consensus; time delay before it becomes an official standard; necessity to adapt the model to specific needs) of international collaboration.
See also **3.6**.

11. JISC/Publishers' Association Working Group and Joint Working Parties.
<http://www.jisc.ac.uk/curriss/collab/c6_pub/#rem_mem>

Initially set up with a fairly broad mandate to discuss issues of mutual concern between libraries and publishers, the enhanced mutual understanding between these two groups has been of great benefit in helping to foster co-operation and collaboration in digital preservation as well as other issues. A number of joint working groups have subsequently been established, including one on the development of model licences and another on long-term retention of digital publications. Model licences based on the initial JISC/PA model licence have been developed to ease the administrative burden imposed by multiple terms and conditions. The latter are being adapted by the Cedars project to deal with digital preservation issues.

12. Working Together: A Workshop for Archivists, Records Managers and Information Technologists. Sponsored by the Coalition for Networked Information (CNI) and Committee on Institutional Co-operation (CIC), 18-19 November 1999.
<http://www.cni.org/projects/working.together>

This is the second workshop in an innovative mechanism for overcoming communication barriers between different professional groups. The purpose of the workshop is "to promote the inclusion of archival and records management issues in systems development projects, create incentives for supporting electronic records management concerns, remove organizational barriers that prevent archivists from implementing electronic records programs, and educate archivists and information technologists about their shared responsibilities and interests in preservation of and access to electronic records. Through collaboration among information professionals, we hope to realize these goals."

13. Bernbom, G, Lippincott, J. and Eaton, F. (1999). 'Working Together: New Collaborations Among Information Professionals.' Cause/Effect 22 (2).
<http://www.educause.edu/ir/library/html/cem9922.html>

14. Berthon, H. and Webb, C. (2000). 'The Moving Frontier: Archiving, Preservation and Tomorrow's Digital Heritage.' Paper presented at VALA 2000 – 10th VALA Biennial Conference and Exhibition, Melbourne, Victoria, 16-18 February 2000.
<http://www.nla.gov.au/nla/staffpaper/hberthon2.html>

15. Dempsey, L. (1999). 'Scientific, Industrial, and Cultural Heritage: a shared approach.' Ariadne 22, December.
<http://www.ariadne.ac.uk/issue22/dempsey>

16. Digital Archiving: Bringing Issues and Stakeholders Together. An Interactive workshop sponsored by ICSTI and ICSU Press. UNESCO House, Paris, 30-31 January 2000.
<http://www.icsti.org/icsti/2000workshop/index.html>

17. McGovern, T.J. and Samuels, H.W. (1997). 'Our Institutional Memory at Risk: Collaborators to the Rescue.' CAUSE/EFFECT 20 (3).
<http://www.educause.edu/ir/library/html/cem9735.html>

18. van der Werf-Davelaar, T. (1999). 'Long-term Preservation of Electronic Publications; the NEDLIB Project'. D-Lib Magazine 5 (9).
<http://www.dlib.org/dlib/september99/vanderwerf/09vanderwerf.html>

3.2 Outreach

Promotional activities are becoming an increasingly important aspect of the business of cultural institutions in general. In terms of digital preservation, there are compelling reasons to engage in an active awareness-raising campaign and programme of outreach activities:

- Preservation is heavily dependent on data creators, funders, and other stakeholders and their actions early in the lifecycle.
- Outreach is cost-effective if it reduces or eliminates the need for retrospective construction of documentation, rights clearance, file re-formatting to a technology neutral format, and other resource intensive interventions by archiving institutions.
- Both the increasing importance of digital information and the need to retain significant digital resources over time need to be actively promoted.
- Awareness raising of the challenges associated with ensuring digital preservation is needed.
- Awareness raising of the resource implications is needed.
- Roles and responsibilities need to be established.
- The overall understanding of the many and varied issues needs to be improved.
- The prospects for effective collaboration based on shared understanding of the issues will be improved.

There is a basic conundrum in attempting to communicate about digital preservation issues. While the overall approach to digital preservation is based on common sense and sound business practices, the subtleties and interdependencies of many of the issues makes it difficult to convey them. Added to this is the current work environment of information overload in which staff have neither the time nor the inclination to undertake research into current trends and master highly technical material.

The combination of these factors makes the danger of misunderstandings far greater in the digital environment. An effective outreach strategy can do much to minimise this danger. As with **3.1**, a high initial investment of resources is likely to yield considerable long-term benefits. The web provides both the incentive and a useful means to promote outreach activities and a number of organisations have made good use of it to disseminate information on digital preservation.

Exemplars and Further Reading

The following are a few examples of outreach activities and are indicative of the wide range of mechanisms which can be used in this context:

1. Feeney, M. (ed). (1999). Digitising Culture: maximising the nation's investment. The National Preservation Office, London.
   Also available online at:
   <http://www.ukoln.ac.uk/services/elib/papers/other/jisc-npo-dig/intro.html>

   The JISC/NPO Digital Archiving Working Group commissioned this publication as a means of making the series of commissioned reports on various aspects of digital preservation more readily accessible to a larger audience.

2. National Library of Canada. Consultation on Online Publications. January 31 2000.
   <http://www.nlc-bnc.ca/bulletin/2000/jun2000e/01e.htm>

   A Consultation on Online Publications was hosted by the National Library of Canada in January 2000 with the purpose of identifying and addressing issues with respect to acquisition, preservation and provision of access to online publications.

3. Arts and Humanities Data Service (AHDS) website. Managing Digital Publications.
   <http://ahds.ac.uk/manage/manintro.html>

   The AHDS invests significant effort in a range of publications and training activities designed to raise awareness of digital preservation issues and provide practical advice to data creators and potential future depositors.

4. Preserving Access to Digital Information (PADI) website.
   <http://www.nla.gov.au/padi>

5. Public Record Office. EROS (Electronic Records in Office Systems) programme.
   <http://www.pro.gov.uk/recordsmanagement/eros>

   The Public Record Office promotes information about its EROS programme via its website and also has a dedicated staff team specifically for outreach activities to government departments.

6. Into the Future: On the Preservation of Knowledge in the Electronic Age
   <http://www.clir.org/pubs/film/film.html>

   The Council for Library and Information Resources (CLIR) and the American Council of Learned Societies produced a film on the subject of digital preservation, Into the Future: On the Preservation of Knowledge on the Electronic Age, as well as an accompanying discussion guide and a compendium of other resources. The purpose was to inform a variety of communities about issues of preservation in the electronic age, to articulate what might be at stake for society, and to point to ways that individuals and groups can work together to find solutions to the challenges posed.

3.3 Third Party Services

Outsourcing specific tasks or services is by no means a new phenomenon. Libraries and archives have contracted out some of their operations for decades. This is an area in which lessons learned from outsourcing in other media can be of value. For example, preservation microfilming has frequently been outsourced and valuable (and sometimes painful) experience has been gained as a result. A major learning experience from preservation microfilming which is directly applicable to the digital environment is the critical importance of having sufficient knowledge of the technology to be able to prepare effective specifications. Earlier microfilming tended to be of poor quality, reinforcing user resistance to it. In recent years, the increased practical experience of the preservation microfilming community has led to the adoption of appropriate standards developed in partnership between the preservation community and the micrographics industry, as well as greatly improved contracts with bureaux. These developments have yielded major benefits for the preservation of the original materials, for users of microfilmed material, and for the cost-effective deployment of scarce preservation resources. The lessons from preservation microfilming were often learned through a process of trial and error but can now serve as an effective reminder to transfer them to the digital environment.

Cost will clearly be a key consideration when deciding whether or not to contract out digital preservation but there are also other factors to consider and the advantages and disadvantages of each will need to be balanced against the overall mission of the institution. For example, legal provisions due to privacy or confidentiality may influence whether outsourcing is appropriate or not. It should also be emphasised that the extent to which the potential advantages of using third party services can be maximised and the potential disadvantages minimised will be heavily dependent on dedicating staff resources to the following:

* Establishing clear and realistic requirements;
* Maintaining good communication between the contractor and the institution;
* Undertaking quality assurance checks;
* Developing and monitoring the contract.

These costs will need to be added to the overall contract costs when calculating the cost benefit of using third party services for digital preservation, bearing in mind that most of these costs will be or should be incurred even if preservation is not outsourced.

Institutional Strategies

Figure 2
Issues and Potential Advantages and Disadvantages of Using
Third Party Services in Digital Preservation Activities

Issue	Potential advantage of using 3rd party services	Potential disadvantage of using 3rd party services
Limited practical experience in preserving complex digital objects over time	• Avoids the need to develop costly infrastructure (particularly important for small institutions) • Allows the institution to focus on other aspects of service provision • Provides specialist skills and experience which may not be available within the institution • If there are economies of scale, outsourcing may well be cost effective • Allows action to be taken in the short to medium term, pending development of infrastructure	• Without some practical experience and expertise, it will be difficult to develop and monitor effective contracts • Without practical experience it will also be difficult effectively to communicate the requirements of the organisation (or to assess whether they are technically feasible or not) • Danger of either not developing or losing skills base • There is no established bench marking. It is still too new an area • Risk of business failure • Until the market increases there may be an over-dependence on one contractor • Unless there are adequate exit strategies, may be locked into an outsourcing contract longer than intended
Access considerations	• Monitoring usage may be more efficient (assuming the contractor has a demonstrated ability to deliver meaningful usage statistics) • There may be synergies and cost savings in outsourcing access and preservation together	• Difficult to control response times which may be unacceptably low and/or more costly, especially for high-use items
Rights Management	• Avoids what is often a resource intensive activity for the institution	• May significantly increase the cost of the contract and/or complicate negotiations with rights holders
Security	• Contract can guarantee security arrangements required by the institution	• Lack of control, especially for sensitive material
Quality control	• A watertight contract will build in stringent quality control requirements	• Risk of loss or distortion may still be unacceptably high for highly significant and/or sensitive material

Exemplars and Further Reading

Digital reformatting

1. RLG tools for beginning digital reformatting projects (1998)
   <http://www.rlg.ac.uk/preserv/RLGtools.html>

   Includes Worksheet for Estimating Digital Reformatting Costs; RLG Guidelines
   for Creating a Proposal for Digital Imaging; RLG Model Request for Information
   (RFI); RLG Model Request for Proposal (RFP).

2. Higher Education Digitisation Service (HEDS).
   <http://heds.herts.ac.uk>

   HEDS provides a host of information on their website and also undertake
   consultancy services for digitisation projects.

Data recovery

3. Ross, Seamus and Gow, Ann. (1999). Digital Archaeology: Rescuing Neglected and
   Damaged Data Resources.
   <http://www.hatii.arts.gla.ac.uk/Projects/BrLibrary/rosgowrt.pdf>
   Appendix 3 refers to a list of Data Recovery companies

Tendering for digital storage systems

4. National Library of Australia. Digital Services Project. Request for Tender –
   Digital Collection Management System.
   <http://www.nla.gov.au/dsp/rft>

   The NLA does not propose this as a model but it is very instructive to any other
   organisation contemplating developing the infrastructure for managing and
   preserving digital collections. The Draft Contract at Attachment 1 clearly includes
   elements specific to Australian Government requirements but also includes many
   generic elements applicable to similar organisations in any country.

Institutional Strategies

3.4 Rights Management

As outlined in **2.2.3**, it is important that copyright and any other intellectual property rights in digital resources to be preserved are clearly identified and access conditions agreed with the depositor and/or rights holders. If the legal ownership of these rights is unclear or excessively fragmented it may be impossible to preserve the materials, or for any users to access them. Rights management should therefore be addressed as part of collection development and accession procedures and be built in to institutional strategies for preservation. The degree of control or scope for negotiation institutions will have over rights will vary but in most cases institutional strategies in this area will help guide operational procedures. It will also be a crucial component of any preservation metadata (see **4.4**) and access arrangements (see **4.5**).

Negotiating rights

As the volume of electronic materials grows and the complexity of rights and number of rights holders in electronic media continues to expand, ad hoc negotiation between preservation agencies and depositors and between rights holders themselves becomes more onerous and less efficient. Development of model letters for staff clearing rights, model deposit agreements, and model licences and clauses covering preservation related activities help to streamline and simplify such negotiations. Institutions should seek assistance from a legal advisor in drafting such models and providing guidance for staff on implementation or permissible variations in negotiations with rights holders.

A number of institutions have developed models which can be adopted or adapted for specific institutions and requirements. The procedures outlined below are a synthesis of sound practices now being promulgated.

Recommended procedures
*   Use a legal advisor to guide your rights management policy and develop documents.
*   Develop model letters for rights clearance, model deposit agreements, model licences and clauses for preservation activities.
*   If you are licensing material from third parties ensure they have addressed future access to subscribed material in the licence and have robust procedures to support this.
*   Prepare reasoned arguments and explanations for your preservation activities. Remember awareness of preservation issues may be low and external stakeholders such as rights holders will need to be convinced of the need and persuaded that their interests will be safeguarded.
*   Keep detailed records of rights negotiations.

- Treat licences and rights correspondence as key institutional records to be retained in fireproof and secure environments.
- Make a schedule clearly identifying a list of materials deposited and covered by the licence. This will ensure that all that is believed to have been sent by the depositor has been received and may form the basis of an acknowledgement of receipt.

Summary of issues for licences and deposit agreements

The following provides a brief checklist and summary of legal issues listed in **2.2.3** which may need to be considered in relation to licences for preservation or deposit agreements for digital materials. Requirements will differ between institutions, sectors and countries and the list should be adapted to individual requirements. This list does not constitute legal advice and you must seek legal counsel for your specific circumstances.

IPR and digital preservation

A clause should be drafted to cover the following:
- Permissions needed for content.
- Permissions needed for associated software.
- Permissions needed for copying for the purposes of preservation.
- Permissions needed for future migration of content to new formats for the purposes of preservation.
- Permissions needed for emulation for the purposes of preservation.
- Permissions in respect of copyright protection mechanisms.

Access
- Permissions and conditions in respect of access to the material.

Statutory and contractual issues
- Statutory permissions and legal deposit obligations in respect of electronic materials.
- Grant and contractual obligations in respect of electronic materials.
- Conditions, rights and appropriate interests of authors, publishers and other funders.
- Confidential information and protection of the confidentiality of individuals and institutions.
- Protecting the integrity and reputation of data creators or other stakeholders.

Investment by the preservation agency
- IPR in any value added by the preservation agency.
- Withdrawal clauses (and associated fees).

Institutional Strategies

Exemplars and Further Reading

1. Arts and Humanities Data Service. Rights Management Framework.
    <http://www.ahds.ac.uk/rights.htm>

    A rights management framework for the AHDS which incorporates model
    agreements for depositors and users to access data.

2. Beagrie, N. and Greenstein, D. (1998). Managing Digital Collections: AHDS Policies,
    Standards and Practices. Consultation draft. Version 1. 15 December 1998.
    <http://www.ahds.ac.uk/managing.htm>

    A handbook of AHDS policies, standards and practices including procedures for
    the administration of the rights management framework.

3. Book Industry Communication, The Rights Decision Tree, Sally Morris and the
    Rights Metadata Working Party.
    <http://www.bic.org.uk/rightree.rtf>

    A model decision tree developed for publishers to administer permissions.
    Although not encompassing digital preservation, it provides a useful guide to the
    concerns of and procedures followed by publishers.

4. Essex Data Archive, Guide to Depositing Data.
    <http://www.data-archive.ac.uk/depositingData/introduction.asp>

    A guide and forms for depositors with the Essex Data Archive. This includes a
    pro forma licence agreement.

5. National Library of Australia. Voluntary Deposit Scheme for Physical Format
    Electronic Publications.
    <http://www.nla.gov.au/policy/vdelec.html>

    A guide to the Voluntary Deposit Scheme for Physical Format Electronic
    Publications in Australia. This includes a pro forma deposit deed.

6. Seville, C. and Weinberger, E. Intellectual Property Rights lessons from the
    CEDARS project for digital preservation. Eighth draft, 1 June 2000.
    <http://www.leeds.ac.uk/cedars/contentpub.htm>

    A draft guide being developed by the CEDARS project.

7. LIBLICENSE. Licensing Digital Information. A Resource for Librarians.
    <http://www.library.yale.edu/~llicense/index.shtml> or UK mirror site:
    <http://mirrored.ukoln.ac.uk/lib-license/index.shtml>

    Web pages and discussion lists to assist librarians in negotiating licence
    agreements. Includes many model licences and publishers' agreements.

8. AHDS and TASI, Copyright FAQ.
   <http://www.tasi.ac.uk/faq/copyrightfaq.html>

9. Bide, M. et al. (1999). Digital Preservation: an introduction to standards issues surrounding the deposit of non-print publications.
   <http://www.bic.org.uk/digpres.doc>

10. Koelman, K. J. et al. (1998). Copyright Aspects of the Preservation of Electronic Publications. Instituut voor Informatierecht Report 7.
    <http://www.ivir.nl/Publicaties/koelman/KBeng2.doc>

11. Lyons, P. (ed). (1998). The JISC/TLTP Copyright Guidelines. (ISBN 1 900508 41 9)
    <http://www.ukoln.ac.uk/services/elib/papers/other>

12. PADI Website. Rights Management.
    <http://www.nla.gov.au/padi/topics/28.html>

3.5 Staff Training and Development

"It isn't simply a case of sending people on courses. There needs to be a fundamental shift." Case Study Interviewee

Carefully designed staff training and continuous professional development can play a key role in successfully making the transition from the traditional model of libraries and archives to the digital or hybrid model. Ensuring all staff have adequate IT skills is only a part of the preparation required for equipping staff to maximise the potential of digital technology. A useful starting point for any organisation is to conduct a skills audit tailored to the needs of the specific institution. The following section is intended to prompt thought and discussion on the various factors which need to be considered before an effective training programme can be developed.

The current work environment is characterised by:
- Rapid and ongoing change.
- Blurring of boundaries within and between institutions.
- Uncertainty in terms of the ability confidently to predict future trends and requirements.
- Less clearly defined and/or changing roles and responsibilities.
- Increased emphasis on collaboration and team work.
- Increased emphasis on accountability.

Senior management are also subject to the same pressures of dealing with what often seems like a moving target and must simultaneously decide on the strategic way forward while ensuring their staff are able to come with them.

As well as threats there are of course huge opportunities and intelligent training and development can do much to minimise the former and unlock the latter. A creative approach to training and development (as opposed to just "sending people on courses") is likely to make a significant difference by:
- Effectively exploiting the technology to improve the overall quality of service.
- Enhancing the individual level of job satisfaction and commitment.
- Improving the strategic outlook for the organisation as a whole.

In terms of digital preservation, there are specific challenges which can be added to the general work environment list above:
- There is little in the way of formal guidance. A certain amount of "learning by doing" is needed, albeit within the context of much important ongoing research and practice in other institutions. Formal and informal co-operation with colleagues working in similar areas is also relevant here. (See also **3.1**).
- Lack of training courses and professional development covering the full range of competencies, skills and knowledge required for digital preservation. A suite of skills and competencies are needed and it may be necessary either

to commission tailor-made training packages and/or utilise off-the-shelf courses which consider individual issues of relevance to digital preservation, e.g. IT skills; copyright; project management; and metadata.

- Little empirical data on costs. This may need a combination of some educated guesses, based on current research, combined with specially designed workshops facilitated by experienced practitioners.

The success of training and development programmes will be affected by the degree to which various roles and responsibilities mesh.

Roles and responsibilities of the institution

- Developing an Information Strategy which integrates IT training with the overall mission of the institution.
- Identifying, in consultation with key staff, a skills audit, to determine what specific competencies are required to meet organisational objectives.
- Establishing a balance between recruiting specific skills and effectively developing existing talent.
- Providing adequate resources for training and development.
- Ensuring staff have access to appropriate equipment.
- Ensuring access to practical "hands on" training and practice.
- Encouraging networking between colleagues in other institutions.
- Considering strategies such as short-term secondment to an institution which may have more experience in a specific area.
- Involving staff in designing training and development programmes.
- Facilitating effective multi-disciplinary communication.
- Taking a broad view of what constitutes training and development (i.e. combination of formal courses, both generic and tailor-made, informal training within the organisation, skills transfer within the organisation, networking etc.).

Roles and responsibilities of professional associations

- Responsiveness to current training and development needs.
- Ability to work with institutions to develop training packages to meet their needs.

Roles and responsibilities of the individual

- Ability to tolerate frequent change.
- Ability to be flexible.
- Ability to work in teams.
- Ability actively to pursue personal professional development through a range of mechanisms.
- Ability to share skills and expertise.
- Ability to learn new skills.
- Ability to apply new skills.

Exemplars and Further Reading

1. Arts and Humanities Data Service. User Support and Training page.
   <http://ahds.ac.uk/users.htm>

2. Edwards, C. (1997). 'Change and Uncertainty in Academic Libraries.' Ariadne, Issue 11.
   <http://www.ariadne.ac.uk/issue11/main>

3. Garrod, P. (1998). 'Skip (Skills for new Information Professionals).' Ariadne, Issue 16.
   <http://www.ariadne.ac.uk/issue16/skip/intro.html>

4. Jefcoate, G. (1997). 'Training for a national library website: the experience of the
   British Library.' Gabriel workshop, session V – Human Resources and Training.
   <http://www.bl.uk/gabriel/en/workshop/ses5-gj.htm>

5. Public Record Office. (1999). Human Resources in Records Management. Kew:
   Public Record Office.
   <http://www.pro.gov.uk/recordsmanagement/standards/humanres.pdf>

6. Ross, S., Moss, M. and Richmond, L. (1998). 'Planning and Designing a Programme
   of Digital Preservation Studies'. In Electronic Access: Archives in the New
   Millenium. Kew: Public Record Office. pp102-110.

7. SKIP (Skills for New Information Professionals) Project. Final Report. 1998.
   <http://www.ukoln.ac.uk/services/elib/papers/other/skip/finalpt2.html>

8. Wettengel, M. (1998). 'Core Competencies for Electronic Record Keeping'. In
   Electronic Access: Archives in the New Millenium. Kew: Public Record Office.
   pp.96-101.

Standards

Using file format standards (see **chapter 5**) and encouraging best practice in data creation and preparation of digital resources for deposit has been a key part of many digital preservation programmes. Combined with collaboration and outreach (see **3.1** and **3.2**) it can be an effective method of addressing some other challenges in digital preservation.

The use and development of reliable standards has long been a cornerstone of the information industry. Their existence facilitates the discovery and sharing of resources. Standards are also relevant to the digital environment and provide the same prospects for resource discovery and interoperability between diverse systems.

There are also specific advantages in terms of digital preservation:
* Standard formats are likely to present fewer problems in migrating from one format to another.
* A relatively small number of standard formats will be much easier to manage in both the short and long term.
* A broad consensus on standards will facilitate and simplify collaboration on digital archiving between institutions and sectors.

While undeniably important, there are also factors which inhibit the use of standards as a digital preservation strategy:
* The pace of change is so rapid that standards which have reached the stage of being formally endorsed – a process which usually takes years – will inevitably lag behind developments and may even be superseded. For example, the DLM Guidelines[1] divides standards into three levels, de facto, publicly available specifications, and de jure, acknowledging the rapidly changing environment.
* Competitive pressures between suppliers encourage the development of proprietary extensions to, or implementations of, standards, which can dilute the advantages of consistency and interoperability for preservation.
* The standards themselves adapt and change to new technological environments, leading to a number of variations of the original standard which may or may not be interoperable long-term even if they are backwards compatible in the short-term.
* Standards can be resource intensive to implement.
* In such a changeable and highly distributed environment, it is impossible to be completely prescriptive.

The above factors mean that standards will need to be seen as part of a suite of preservation strategies rather than the key strategy itself. The digital environment is far less inclined to be constrained by rigid rules of any kind and recent years have witnessed a change of emphasis, from reliance on standards towards establishing common approaches which are sufficiently flexible to adapt to both changing circumstances and individual requirements.

Best practice

The necessity for a more fluid approach has led to increased efforts to establish best practice. Increasingly this is being refined into concepts of "ideal practice", "acceptable practice", and "unacceptable practice" to aid implementation. There is still some distance to go before best practice in all aspects of digital preservation can be definitively articulated and in such a rapidly changing environment it may never be categorically established. There are beginning to emerge common approaches based on increasing practical involvement with the many and varied issues. For example, NEDLIB, Cedars, the British Library, and the National Library of Australia have all either adopted the OAIS Reference Model or have taken account of it in their system specifications. There are also increased efforts to define a whole range of acceptable practices, particularly in the creation of digital resources (see also **4.1**), many of which will significantly assist later digital preservation efforts. This guidance invariably includes, but is not limited to, the use of appropriate standards.

Common elements of good practice in creation include:
* The use of open, non-proprietary data formats.
* Providing metadata in conformance with emerging standards and documentation aimed at facilitating future use and future management of the resource.
* Assigning permanent names to online digital resources.

References

1. DLM Forum. (1997). Guidelines on Best Practice for Using Electronic Information. <http://europa.eu.int/ISPO/dlm/documents/gdlines.pdf>

Exemplars and Further Reading

1. Arts and Humanities Data Service. Guides to Good Practice.
   <http://www.ahds.ac.uk/guides.htm>

2. Beagrie, N. and Greenstein, D. (1998). Managing Digital Collections: AHDS
   Policies, Standards and Practices. Consultation draft. Version 1. 15 December 1998.
   <http://www.ahds.ac.uk/managing.htm>

3. DLM Forum. (1997). Guidelines on Best Practice for Using Electronic
   Information.
   <http://europa.eu.int/ISPO/dlm/documents/gdlines.pdf>

4. Gatenby, P. (2000). 'Digital Archiving – Developing Policy and Best Practice
   Guidelines at the National Library of Australia.' Paper presented at an interactive
   Workshop on Digital Archiving sponsored by ICSTI and ICSU Press, 30-31
   January 2000. UNSECO House, Paris
   <http://www.icsti.org/icsti/2000workshop/gatenby.html>

5. NOF-digitise Technical Standards and Guidelines. Version One; June 2000.
   <http://www.peoplesnetwork.gov.uk/nof/technicalstandards.html>

6. Reference Model for an Open Archival Information System (OAIS) Draft
   Recommendation for Space Data Systems (CCSDS), CCSDS 650.0-R-1, May 1999.
   <http://www.ccsds.org/RP9905/RP9905.html>

   It is also instructive to look at responses to the draft OAIS model from
   the perspective of deposit libraries which have reviewed or implemented it.
   See, for example the National Library of Australia's response at:
   <http://www.nla.gov.au/wgroups/oais>

   NEDLIB contribution to the review of OAIS is at:
   <http:///www.kb.nl/coop/nedlib/results/OAISreviewbyNEDLIB.html>

7. PADI Website. Data Documentation & Standards.
   <http://www.nla.gov.au/padi/topics/29.html>

8. Public Record Office. (1999). Management, Appraisal and Preservation of
   Electronic Records. Volume 1, Principles & Volume 2, Procedures.
   <http://www.pro.gov.uk/recordsmanagement/eros/guidelines>

9. Public Record Office Victoria (Australia). (2000). Standard for the Management
   of Electronic Records in the Victorian Government. Version 1.0, April 2000.
   (PROS 99/007).
   <http://www.pro.vic.gov.au/gservice/standard/pros9907.htm>

4   Organisational Activities

Intended primary audience

Creators and publishers of digital resources, third-party service providers, operational managers and staff with responsibility for implementing institutional activities of relevance to digital preservation. It is assumed that these will include a) staff from structurally separate parts of the organisation, and b) a wide range of knowledge of digital preservation, from novice to sophisticated; c) both technical and non technical perspectives; d) a wide range of functional activities with a direct or indirect link to digital preservation activities.

Assumed level of knowledge of digital preservation

Wide-ranging, from novice to advanced.

Purpose

- To provide pointers to sources of advice and guidance aimed at encouraging good practice in creating and managing digital materials. The importance of the creator in facilitating digital preservation is stressed throughout the handbook but particularly in **4.1**. Good practice in digitisation and other digital materials creation is crucial to the continued viability of digital materials.
- To raise awareness of factors which need to be considered when creating or acquiring digital materials.
- To provide pointers to helpful sources of advice and guidance for both novices and those who have already begun to think through the implications of digital technology on their operational activities.

4.1   Creating Digital Materials

"The first line of defense against loss of valuable digital information rests with the creators, providers and owners of digital information."[1]

The Task Force on Archiving of Digital Information articulated one of the earliest acknowledgements of the crucial role of the creator in helping to ensure long-term access to the digital resources they create. This view has been reiterated in many other documents since the Final Report of the Task Force was published. Clearly, most individual creators cannot be expected to take on long-term commitment to preserving the digital content they create[2]. Every digital resource has a life cycle and different stakeholders and interests within this. However, it is both achievable and highly desirable that a dialogue is established between them when issues of long-term preservation are involved. Given the crucial role of the creator in undertaking short to medium-term preservation and at least facilitating medium to long-term preservation, this section will focus on encouraging good practice in creation of digital materials which will assist in their future management.

A major source of current activity and investment is in the digitisation of analogue materials, in particular digital imaging. There are many useful tools which provide assistance with various stages of digitisation projects. This section of the handbook will not attempt to duplicate work done by others by producing a detailed decision tree for digitisation but will act as a means of flagging issues relevant to the management of digital objects and provide links to more detailed sources of advice and guidance.

There is also a wide range of digitisation methods and this section is not intended as a digitisation guide or manual for different methods of capturing information. Our focus remains the implications for digital preservation in the creation process. Two areas have been selected, creating digital surrogates and creating electronic records as being of most widespread interest and illustrating general preservation principles for other data creation methods.

The emphasis on digitisation in this section reflects its current importance as increasing numbers of institutions embark on digitising parts of their collections. It is important to reinforce that this handbook is not considering the potential of digitisation as a preservation reformatting tool. The emphasis throughout the handbook is on the preservation of "born digital" materials, or the products of digitisation (the digital surrogates themselves), not the preservation of the analogue originals.

Many digitisation projects cite enhanced access as the major objective, a perfectly legitimate objective but unless due care and attention is given to how that access can be maintained over time, it may well be short-lived. This section of the handbook makes the assumption that it is highly unlikely that all current digitisation initiatives are being undertaken with due regard to the long-term viability of the digital surrogates they are creating. A related assumption is that it would be useful to encourage good practice in creating digital materials and to point to existing sources of guidance.

A second major source of current activity is in the creation of electronic records. This section is divided into two, the first focusing on the creation of digital surrogates through digitisation and the second on the creation of electronic records. Both have excellent sources of advice and guidance and key references are provided in an annotated reading list following the section.

Organisational Activities

4.1.1 Creating Digital Surrogates

The following diagram (Figure 3) illustrates how the relationships between the various elements should ideally flow within an institution. For the sake of simplicity, the diagram looks at the broad issues as they apply to long-term preservation, referring to more detailed guidance documents, as appropriate. It suggests that a strong corporate presence, in the form of policies and associated strategies, is required in order to provide the necessary guidance and authority to staff involved in institutional digitisation projects. Consideration of how the digital surrogates will be maintained needs to be made as early as possible, preferably at the design stage. It is also important to note that the broad model applies to all activities, not just digitisation, and the Further Reading section reflects this wider perspective.

Figure 3
Creating Digital Surrogates – Management Context and Checklist

Corporate Policies

Outlining broad policy towards selection for digitisation, purposes of digitisation; management of digital surrogates etc. Should also indicate responsibility.

See Further Reading for models and frameworks and checklist for elements which may need to be addressed in policy.

Corporate Strategies

Strategies to put into practice the principles articulated in corporate policy statements. See Further Reading for models and frameworks and checklist below for issues needing to be considered.

Corporate Procedures

Guidelines for operational activities which are clearly linked to corporate strategies. See checklist below for elements which need to be considered.

4.1.2 Creating Electronic Records

Most records created during the day-to-day work that takes place in the public and private sector are now created electronically. Increasingly, they will also be distributed and accessed electronically. In the UK, the recent white paper, Modernising Government [7] aims to have all newly created public records electronically stored and retrieved by 2004 and a strategy has now been developed to achieve this aim. Combined with recent legislation on Data Protection and Freedom of Information [8], this makes efficient and effective management of electronic records of pressing concern. Records management is a key aspect of the Freedom of Information Bill and a code of practice to be issued by the Lord Chancellor will underpin the Act [9]. In order to fulfil their legal and accountability responsibilities, organisations in the UK will need to ensure they plan for efficient and effective electronic records management (ERM). There are also organisational implications (See also **2.2** and **Chapter 4** for more discussion of these issues).

Three major sources of guidance have been consulted for this section. They are:

- Electronic Records Management: Framework for Information Age Government. March 2000.
  <http://www.e-envoy.gov.uk/publications/frameworks/erm/erm.htm>

- DLM Forum. (1997). Guidelines on the Best Practices for Using Electronic Information.
  <http://europa.eu.int/ISPO/dlm/documents/gdlines.pdf>

- Public Record Office. (1999). Guidelines on the Management, Appraisal and Preservation of Electronic Records. Volumes 1 (Principles) and 2 (Procedures). Kew: Public Record Office.
  <http://www.pro.gov.uk/recordsmanagement/eros/guidelines>

There is a commonality of themes in these three sources and the following checklist draws heavily on all three.

Formal corporate policies.
"It needs to be clearly understood across the department that everyone is responsible in some way for records and that responsible behaviour is implanted throughout all relevant operational activities. Establishment of a defining framework of formal corporate policies on electronic records is one principal means of helping to achieve this goal." [10]

As in the previous section on digitising analogue collections, it is difficult to overemphasise the importance of corporate policies promulgated throughout the organisation and re-visited at regular intervals to ensure continuing relevance in a rapidly changing environment. The Public Record

Checklist[3]

Issues in Preserving Digital Surrogates

	Checklist	Issues in Preserving Digital Surrogates
1	Assessment of need for digitisation	Has the material already been digitised? If so, is it to an appropriate standard and readily accessible?
2	Finding funds for the project	What archiving policies exist, both from the funding agency (if externally funded) and the institution with prime responsibility for the project?
3	Planning the project and assigning resources	Need to set aside recurrent funds for maintenance of the digital copies as well as one-off funds for conversion. Ensure all relevant stakeholders are aware of the project (for example, if another part of the organisation or an external agency is expected to maintain the resource, they will need to be included in discussions at this point, if not before)
4	Selection of materials	Copyright. Need to ensure permission is given both to digitise the original and to make copies of the digital copy for the purposes of preservation. For further information, see 2.2.3. Legal Issues and 3.4. Rights Management. Condition and completeness of original. Is it capable of being re-scanned at a later date if the digital copy is lost?
5	Decide how the information content needs to be organised (for example, searchable text databases and/or document page images)	Selection of appropriate file formats and storage media for both master/archive copies and derivatives.
6	Decide digitisation method appropriate to analogue original and goals of the project.	Details of the digitisation method need to be documented and attached to the metadata record to enable future management.
7	Preparing originals for digitisation	Documentation. Will the originals be retained? (if scanning paper records, the PRO advises not to take any action on discarding the originals until it is established that a) the electronic version is legally admissible and/or b) the electronic version is capable of long-term preservation[4].) For collection material, Kenney and Chapman provide a decision tree

for deciding whether or not to retain the originals post-digitisation[5]. The latter will of course not be an issue for projects digitising valuable treasures within a collection, the main issue then will be whether or not the original is too fragile to be re-scanned at a later date if the digital copy is lost. In any of these cases, if the digital copy becomes the primary means of access, it will be subject to the same requirements as born digital material.

8 Conversion

Documentation of technical characteristics. Compression algorithm (if used); bit depth required; scanning resolution etc. Create backup copies as soon as conversion is undertaken.

9 Quality assurance checks

Digital surrogate needs to be of an acceptable preservation quality.
If using third party services, need to ensure documentation clarifies responsibility for quality assurance.

10 Final indexing and cataloguing

Metadata for resource discovery and for managing and preservation of digital copy.

11 Loading data into computer systems

Document storage requirements for access and preservation copies (if different).
Make backup copies as appropriate. Note: the PRO recommends a minimum of four copies as a general rule, with a minimum of two on separate storage media. If the analogue original is in good condition and capable of being re-scanned in case of loss of the digital copy, two copies, each stored geographically separately, may be sufficient[6].

12 Implementing archiving and preservation strategies or transferring to a preservation agency

Required standards for formats, storage media, documentation, and transfer procedures.
Storage of masters and backup copies.
Strategies for media refreshment and changes in technological environment.

Office Guidelines also reinforce the need to ensure that the policy does more than pay "lip service" to accountability requirements:

"Most important of all, a corporate policy must be agreed to. Writing the words of a policy statement is much less difficult than the process of gaining agreement to them …a policy which is ignored is worse than no policy at all."[11]

The policy should address issues such as:
- The status of electronic records within the organisation and broad definitions of what they constitute.
- Broad definition of records which constitute permanent records worthy of long-term preservation.
- Whether long-term management will be undertaken by a third party service provider or in-house.
- Roles and responsibilities within the organisation.

Corporate strategies

The best way to optimise the management of electronic information is to define a coherent global strategy from the outset, ensuring that everyone concerned is involved. One solution is to set up a multidisciplinary team to define and monitor the strategy[12].

The suggestion above recognises the fact that there needs to be a mechanism which will bring together the range of expertise necessary to develop effective strategies. The implicit assumption in monitoring the strategy is also that there will be clearly defined timeframes with achievable targets to monitor.

The following issues should be addressed in corporate strategies and may well require other supporting documents setting out in more details how the strategies can be achieved:
- Authenticity – What organisational and technical strategies will ensure that the electronic record is reliable and legally admissible?
- Appraisal and retention periods – How will they be developed and applied?
- Migrating records worthy of permanent preservation to new systems – How will they remain accessible and usable for as long as they are needed?
- Selection of media and formats – What standards should be used for various categories of electronic documents across the organisation?
- Metadata – How will essential metadata be defined and how can it be ensured that it will remain linked to the corporate record?
- Training and awareness raising for staff – What ongoing training requirements and supporting guidelines are required to support good records management practice?
- Compliance with the corporate policy – How will compliance with the corporate policy be monitored?

Corporate procedures

Procedures developed by the Records and IT Manager need to define:

- The design of the recordkeeping system.
- The types of electronic records which need to be captured by the system.
- What documents need to be captured as records.
- What naming conventions should be used.
- What metadata needs to be kept with the records.

Training and guidance

"New record keeping skills are required in a fully electronic environment of end-users as creators and users of records. They will have more responsibility for correctly identifying and dealing with electronic records at the point of creation, and these shifts imply significant cultural change in attitudes and behaviour towards record-making and use." [13]

Most organisations will need to undergo a cultural shift which places more responsibility on the creators of records than has previously been the case. Staff will need to be aware of the following, through guidelines and training:

- At what point does the document they are working on become a formal record and therefore managed as part of the Electronic Records Management of the organisation?
- What metadata should they provide?
- What naming conventions should they use?

References

1. Waters, D. and Garrett, J. (1996). Preserving Digital Information: Report of the Task Force on Archiving of Digital Information commissioned by the Commission on Preservation and Access and the Research Libraries Group. Washington, DC: Commission on Preservation and Access. p.47.
    <http://www.rlg.org/ArchTF>

2. DLM Forum. (1997). Guidelines on the Best Practices for Using Electronic Information. These make a useful distinction between 'live' and 'frozen' information, where the former is, in general, managed by the creator and the latter by archivists and librarians who need to ensure it remains the same.
    <http://europa.eu.int/ISPO/dlm/documents/gdlines.pdf>

3. Source of checklist: Adapted from Tanner, S. and Lomax-Smith, J. (1999). 'How Much Does It Really Cost?' Paper for DRH '99 Conference.
    <http://heds.herts.ac.uk/resources/papers/drh99.pdf>
    and AHDS 'Digitisation: a Project Planning Checklist'
    <http://www.ahds.ac.uk/checklist.htm>

4. Public Record Office. (1999). Guidelines on the Management, Appraisal and Preservation of Electronic Records. Volume 2: Procedures, p. 17.
    <http://www.pro.gov.uk/recordsmanagement/eros/guidelines>

5. Kenney, A. R. and Chapman, S. (1996). Digital Imaging for Libraries and Archives. New York: Cornell University Library. Figure 1. p.190.

6. A Digital Preservation Strategy for the PRO. 1999. 3.5.3.

7. Modernising Government. March 1999. Cm 4310. Chapter 5.
    <http://www.officialdocuments.co.uk/document/cm43/4310/4310.htm>

8. E-government: a strategic framework for public services in the Information Age.
    <http://www.citu.gov.uk/iagc/pdfs/Strategy.pdf>

9. The FOI bill had been given royal assent in July 2000 and a timeframe of everything being in place within five years of royal assent has been given. A Model Action Plan for Developing Records Management Compliant with the Lord Chancellor's Code of Practice under section 46 of the Freedom of Information Act 2000 is available from the PRO website at
    <http://www.pro.gov.uk/recordsmanagement/access/foiactionplan.pdf>

10. Public Record Office. (1999). Guidelines on the Management, Appraisal and Preservation of Electronic Records. Volumes 1: Principles, p. 17 Kew: Public Record Office.
    <http://www.pro.gov.uk/recordsmanagement/eros/guidelines>

11. Public Record Office. (1999). Guidelines on the Management, Appraisal and Preservation of Electronic Records. Volume 1: Principles, p. 25. Kew: Public Record Office.
<http://www.pro.gov.uk/recordsmanagement/eros/guidelines>

12. DLM Forum. (1997). Guidelines on the Best Practices for Using Electronic Information. p.20.
<http://europa.eu.int/ISPO/dlm/documents/gdlines.pdf>

13. Electronic Records Management: Framework for Information Age Government March 2000.
<http://www.e-envoy.gov.uk/publications/frameworks/erm/erm.htm>

Exemplars and Further Reading

There are numerous excellent sources of guidance covering all aspects of digital materials creation. This is an area where there is not only theoretical guidance but recommendations based on solid practical experience. There is now such a rich source of information relating to creating digital materials, that it is possible to avoid many of the pitfalls experienced by earlier projects. The difficulty, particularly for those new to the task, is in selecting which of the bewildering array of resources best suits a specific need. The purpose of this further reading list is to simplify the task of finding the resource most suited to a particular situation by categorising key guidance documents and supplying sufficient descriptive information to assess their relevance.

Corporate policies and strategies – guidance

1. Beagrie, N. and Greenstein, D. (1998). A Strategic Policy Framework for Creating and Preserving Digital Collections. Version 4.0 (Final Draft). ELib Supporting Study P3. Library Information Technology Centre, South Bank University, London. Also available online at:
   <http://ahds.ac.uk/strategic.htm>

   The study aims to provide a strategic policy framework for the creation and preservation of digital resources, and to develop guidance based on case studies, further literature and ongoing projects which will facilitate effective implementation of the policy framework. The authors advocate the concept of a life-cycle approach in preserving digital resources and suggest that the ability to preserve digital resources into the long-term rest heavily on decisions made at different stages in the life-cycle. Decisions taken during design and creation and those taken when a resource is accessioned into a collection are considered the most influential. Case studies are divided into six categories: data banks; digitisers; funding and other agencies; institutional archives; academic data archives; legal deposit libraries.

2. DLM Forum. (1997). Guidelines on Best Practice for Using Electronic Information.
   <http://europa.eu.int/ISPO/dlm/documents/gdlines.pdf>

   Designed as multidisciplinary guidelines and arising out of the DLM Forum, a European forum which brings together experts from industry, research, administration and archives to discuss issues of mutual concern. The Guidelines are intended to help define short and medium term strategies for managing electronically stored data. Annex 8.4 contains a checklist for an electronic information strategy.

3. Electronic Records Management: Framework for Information Age Government. March 2000.
   <http://www.e-envoy.gov.uk/publications/frameworks/erm/erm.htm>

   Developed to provide guidance to departments which will need to commence working towards the Modernising Government target of all newly created public records being both electronically stored and retrieved by 2004.

4. Hedstrom, M. and Montgomery, S. (1998). Digital Preservation Needs and Requirements in RLG Member Institutions. Mountain View, CA: RLG.
   <http://www.rlg.ac.uk/preserv/digpres.html>

Organisational Activities

71

Fifty-four RLG member institutions were surveyed for this study, including seven in the UK. One of the key questions the study was charged with answering was what policies and practices are being used to preserve digital materials. The report concluded that digital preservation policies are not well developed in member institutions and that " …among those institutions with digital preservation responsibilities, the lack of good models for digital preservation and confusion about the most appropriate methods and approaches are major obstacles to developing effective policies and practices."

5. Public Record Office. (1999). Guidelines on the Management, Appraisal and Preservation of Electronic Records. Volumes 1: Principles, and 2: Procedures. Kew: Public Record Office.
    <http://www.pro.gov.uk/recordsmanagement/eros/guidelines>

    These two publications are part of a series of guidance documents prepared under the auspices of the Electronic Records from Office Systems (EROS) programme of the Public Record Office. Volume 1, Principles, sets the scene for electronic record management and provides broad strategies arising out of the principles. Volume 2: Procedures, provides more detailed guidance for putting the principles into practice. Chapter 5 of this volume contains guidance on how to develop a preservation strategy and advises that the plan must be agreed by three parties, the systems administrator, the records manager, and the budget holder. This advice reinforces the need to a) involve what may well be administratively separate parts of the organisation in the development of an effective strategy (for example, Records and IT Managers) and b) the importance of corporate ownership of the strategy.

6. RLG/DLF Task Force on Policy and Practice for Long-Term Retention of Digital Materials.
    <http://www.rlg.ac.uk/preserv/digrlgdlf99.html>

    This Task Force was formed in response to the findings of the RLG survey (see above Hedstrom and Montgomery, 1998). The model policies and practices gathered by the Task Force relate to three categories of digital object:
    1) institutional records in digital form;
    2) locally digitised materials;
    3) electronic publications.

Corporate policies and guidelines – institutional models

1. Columbia University Libraries. Policy for Preservation of Digital Resources. July 2000.
    <http://www.columbia.edu/cu/libraries/services/preservation/dlpolicy.doc>

    Specifies different categories of digital resources the University accepts responsibility for, including "Digital Resources reformatted by CUL, and deemed to be of long-term value in digital form". Also points to other relevant policy documents, such as Selection Criteria for Digital Imaging Projects
    <http://www.columbia.edu/cu/libraries/digital/criteria.htm>
    and Technical Recommendations for Digital Imaging Projects
    <http://www/columbia.edu/acis/dl/imagespec.html>

2. Library of Congress. Preservation Digital Reformatting Program. 1999.
<http://lcweb.loc.gov/preserv/prd/presdig/presintro.html>

The digitising component of the preservation reformatting program has three
parts, 1) selection criteria, 2) digital reformatting principles and specifications
(includes, for example, retention of analogue version of digitally reformatted
items "…until the Preservation Directorate has confidence that the life-cycle
management of digital data will ensure access for as long as, or longer than, the
analogue version.", 3) life-cycle management of LC digital data (a term used in
preference to digital preservation in order to avoid potential confusion of
definition). As used here, life-cycle management is defined as "the progressive
technology and workflow requirements needed to ensure long-term sustainability
of and accessibility to digital objects and/or metadata."

3. National Library of Australia Digitisation Policy 2000-2004.
<http://www.nla.gov.au/policy/digitisation.html>

Described as "…a guide to both the digitisation of items held by the Library,
and the management of these digital objects". While the policy covers four years,
it includes a stated intention to review it annually. Also includes specific goals
for the first year, which include setting up a Digitisation Steering Committee.

4. National Library of Canada. Networked Electronic Publications Policy and
Guidelines. October 1998.
<http://www.nlc-bnc.ca/9/8/index-e.html>

5. Society of American Archivists. The Preservation of Digitized Reproductions. 1997. Online.
<http://www.archivists.org/statements/digitize.html>

This differs from the models above in that it is intended as advice to institutions,
as opposed to being tailored specifically to an individual institution. As such it
tends to refer to broad principles at a fairly high level. This is probably one of the
earliest explications of the role of the creator as recommended by the US Task
Force. "Responsibility for long-term access to digital archives rests initially with the
creator or owner of the materials. The resource and administrative implications
of this fact cannot be minimized and must play a role in the decision to digitize
archival and manuscript materials."

General guidance – digital resource creation

1. AHDS Guides to Good Practice
<http://www.ahds.ac.uk/guides.htm>

The Arts and Humanities Data Service has produced a series of Guides to Good
Practice to provide the arts and humanities research and teaching communities
with practical instruction in applying recognised standards and good practice in
the creation, preservation and use of digital materials. Some of the titles are
geared towards specific disciplines while others are cross-disciplinary and geared
towards providing general guidance. Titles linked online at 14 June 2001:
1. Archiving Aerial Photography and Remote Sensing Data;
2. Excavation and Fieldwork Archiving;

3. GIS (Geographic Information Systems);
4. Digitising History: a guide to creating digital resources from historical documents;
5. Creating Digital Performance Resources;
6. Creating and Documenting Electronic Texts;
7. Creating Digital Resources for the Visual Arts: Standards and Good Practice;

2. Guides to Quality in Visual Resource Imaging. July 2000.
   <http://www.rlg.ac.uk/visguides>

   The five guides have been commissioned by DLF and CLIR and published with RLG in order to fill a perceived gap. "While resources for instruction in digitizing text or text and images existed and were growing, none specifically addressed the challenges of two- and three-dimensional, as well as color intensive, materials. The five guides are:
   1. Planning an Imaging Project, by Linda Serenson Colet, Museum of Modern Art
   2. Selecting a Scanner, by Don Williams, Eastman Kodak Company
   3. Imaging Systems: the Range of Factors Affecting Image Quality, by Donald D'Amato, Mitretek Systems
   4. Measuring Quality of Digital Masters, by Franziska Frey, Image Permanence Institute, Rochester Institute of Technology
   5. File Formats for Digital Masters, by Franziska Frey.

3. Joint RLG and NPO Preservation Conference on Guidelines for Digital Imaging. 28-30 September 1998.
   <http://www.rlg.org/preserv/joint>>

   Gathers together a number of international experts to discuss the full range of preservation issues associated with digital imaging.

4. Kenney, Anne R. and Chapman, Stephen (1996). Digital Imaging for Libraries and Archives. New York: Cornell University Library. Ordering details online. Available: <http://www.library.cornell.edu/preservation/dila.html>

   This guide won the 1997 Leland Prize from the Society of American Archivists for "writing of superior excellence and usefulness in the field of archival history, theory and practice." The companion volume Moving Theory Into Practice (2000) is cited below.

5. Kenney, Anne R. and Rieger, Oya Y. (2000). Moving Theory Into Practice. Mountain View, CA: Research Libraries Group. (ISBN 0-9700225-0-6)
   Table of Contents and Ordering details online.
   <http://www.rlg.ac.uk/preserv/mtip2000.html>

   The authors have used extensive practical knowledge to provide detailed guidance to institutions contemplating digital conversion of cultural resources.

6. Higher Education Digitisation Service (HEDS).
   <http://heds.herts.ac.uk>
   This JISC funded service provides a full range of services, from advice and consultancy to actual scanning. Their website also contains links to papers prepared by HEDS staff and others.

7. Lee, S. (1999). Scoping the Future of the University of Oxford's Digital Library Collections: Final Report.
    <http://www.Bodley.ox.ac.uk/scoping/report.html>

    The aims of this project were:
*   To document, analyse, and evaluate Oxford's current digitisation activities, as a basis for assessing the effectiveness of the various methodologies used.
*   To investigate the possibilities for building on the existing project-based work and for migrating it into viable services for library users.
*   To develop appropriate selection criteria for creating digital collections in the context of local, national, and international scholarly requirements for digital library products and services.
*   To make recommendations for further investment and activity within the UK research libraries community.

    The resulting report, with ten appendices, is an extremely detailed investigation of a whole range of issues amounting to a strategic plan for the future digital library development of this institution. While specifically designed for one university, the issues are also applicable to many other organisational contexts.

8. NOF-digitise Technical Standards and Guidelines. Version One; June 2000.
    <http://www.peoplesnetwork.gov.uk/nof/technicalstandards.html>

    Stage two of the nof-digitise programme has provided £50 million worth of funding for the creation of digital content for users of the People's network and the national grid for learning. A web-based resource has been provided to support Stage two, providing advice on standards for accessibility, availability, document and file formats, search and request protocols, security and e-commerce, preservation and metadata.

9. Technical Advisory Service for Images (TASI).
    <http://www.tasi.ac.uk>

    A JISC funded service set up to advise and support the academic community on the digital creation, storage and delivery of image-related information. TASI also collaborated with the Visual Arts Data Service (VADS) to produce Creating Digital Resources for the Visual Arts, one of the titles in the AHDS Guides to Good Practice series.

Digitisation: outsourcing versus in-house

Decisions will need to be made on whether to outsource all or part of a digitisation project or to undertake all of it in-house. Some guidance can be found in Kenney and Chapman (1996), Chapter 5, Outsourcing Imaging Services which reviews the pros and cons of outsourcing. Tanner and Lomax-Smith (1999) suggest that while cost is likely to favour outsourcing if large volumes of material are being digitised, other factors, such as whether or not the material can be taken out of the institution, will obviously influence whether in-house digitisation will be the preferred option.

Whatever option is selected, the host institution will still need to commit significant resources to ensuring the project successfully delivers its stated goals.

1. Kenney, Anne R. and Chapman, Stephen (1996). Digital Imaging for Libraries and Archives. New York: Cornell University Library. Ordering details online.
   <http://www.library.cornell.edu/preservation/dila.html>

2. Tanner, S. and Lomax-Smith, J. (1999). 'How Much Does It Really Cost?' Paper for DRH '99 Conference.
   <http://heds.herts.ac.uk/resources/papers/drh99.pdf>

3. RLG Tools for Digital Imaging
   <http://www.rlg.ac.uk/preserv/RLGtools.html>

   RLG Tools for Digital Imaging provide guidance in the form of:
   - A worksheet for Estimating Digital Reformatting Costs.
   - RLG Guidelines for Creating a Request for Proposal.
   - RLG Model RFI (an example of how Cornell University invited vendors that would be interested in receiving their project RFP).
   - RLG Model RFP (an example of how Cornell University adapted the RLG Guidelines for Creating a Request for Proposal for use in a text-based digitisation project).

Guidance on selection for digitisation

1. Ayris, Paul. (1998). 'Guidance for selecting materials for digitisation'. Joint RLG and NPO Preservation Conference: Guidelines for Digital Imaging.
   <http://www.rlg.ac.uk/preserv/joint/ayris.html>

   The paper identifies studies which have considered the role of selection in the process of digitisation and suggests a decision-making matrix of twenty questions grouped around four issues, Assessment; Gains; Standards; Administrative Issues.

2. Lee, S. (1999). Scoping the Future of the University of Oxford's Digital Library Collections: Final Report.
   <http://www.Bodley.ox.ac.uk/scoping/report.html>

   Appendix B is a detailed workflow chart providing assistance in deciding whether or not to proceed with a digitisation project.

3. Hazen, D., Horrell, J. and Merrill-Oldham, J. (1998). Selecting Research Collections for Digitization. Council on Library and Information Resources, August 1998.
   <http://www.clir.org/pubs/reports/reports.html>

   Provides detailed planning information for research libraries contemplating large-scale digital conversion of holdings for research and teaching purposes. Discusses selection criteria, imaging standards, rights management issues, preservation concerns, and impact of digitisation on the library and its users.

Funding

1. The Technical Advisory Service for Images (TASI) maintains a list of potential sources of funding on its website.
   <http://www.tasi.ac.uk/resources/funding.html>

   Note that some of these have specific clauses relating to digital preservation. For example the Arts and Humanities Research Board (AHRB) makes it a condition that for grants awarded where a significant product or by-product is the creation of an electronic resource, it is offered for deposit at the Arts and Humanities Data Service (AHDS) within three months of the end of the project. Both time and adequate funding are provided to prepare the data for deposit (see AHRB Grant Applications and Awards: <http://ahds.ac.uk/applicants.htm>). The New Opportunities Fund (NOF) advises in their Information for Applicants that intellectual property issues and technical standards identified by NOF must be observed (see New Opportunities Fund, information for new applicants at <http://www.nof-digitise.org>).

   The deadlines for responding to calls for proposals may not always mean that it is feasible to include all costs for the project, and in particular for keeping the data but it does need to be acknowledged that this will become a cost to the institution. See also **Costs** on page 79.

Preservation metadata

1. National Archives of Australia. Recordkeeping Metadata Standard for Commonwealth Agencies. May 1999.
   <http://www.naa.gov.au/recordkeeping/control/rkms/summary.html>

2. Bearman, David and Sochats, Ken. (1996). Metadata Requirements for Evidence. Pittsburgh, Pa: University of Pittsburgh School of Information Science.
   <http://www.lis.pitt.edu/~nhprc/BACartic.html>

3. Cedars Project Team and UKOLN. Metadata for Digital Preservation: the Cedars Project Outline Specification. Draft for Public Consultation. March 2000
   <http://www.leeds.ac.uk/cedars>

   This document represents a major aspect of the work of Cedars in the development of a metadata framework which will enable the long-term preservation of digital resources. The outline indicates that it generally adheres to the metadata identified by the Reference Model for an Open Archival Information System (OAIS). The document "starts with the structure provided by the OAIS model and populates it with metadata elements chosen by practical investigation of archiving real digital resources, further refined by comments received from a selective consultation process." It also restricts itself to metadata required for preservation, rather than other processes.

4. Dollar, Charles. (1999). Authentic Electronic Records: Strategies for Long-Term Access. Chicago: Cohasset Associates. (ISBN 0-9700640-0-4)
   Appendix 7. Preservation Metadata Model.

5. National Library of Australia. Draft Preservation Metadata Set. October 1999
    <http://www.nla.gov.au/preserve/pmeta.html>

    This has been developed as part of the NLA's plans for its digital collections.
    The introduction states that "There have been a number of efforts to develop
    metadata specifications and sets to support a wide variety of digital resources.
    Because of its pressing business needs to manage both 'born digital' and 'digital
    surrogate' collections, the National Library of Australia has tried to find, or if
    necessary develop, metadata models to accommodate both." The draft also
    emphasises that the metadata set is intended as a data output model, i.e.
    information required to manage digital collections, not necessarily what data should
    be entered, how it should be entered, by whom, and at what time. Like the Cedars
    specification, this document restricts itself to metadata required for preservation.

6. Public Record Office. (1999). Guidelines on the Management, Appraisal, and
    Preservation of Electronic Records. Volume 2: Principles. Chapter 2.
    <http://www.pro.gov.uk/recordsmanagement/eros/guidelines>

    Defines three classes of metadata: document metadata; record level metadata;
    and file/folder metadata and recommends elements for each.

7. RLG Working Group on Preservation Issues of Metadata; Final Report. May 1998.
    <http://www.rlg.ac.uk/preserv/presmeta.html>

    The Working Group noted that to date, the emphasis of metadata has been on
    resource discovery and retrieval. Taking two prominent metadata systems, Dublin
    Core and the Program for Cooperative Cataloguing's USMARC-based core
    record standard, the group specified those elements not covered by these two
    systems but important to serve the preservation needs of digital masters. The
    group confined itself to digital image files and recommended sixteen data
    elements for this category of digital resource.

    See also **4.4**.

Technical standards

1. Beagrie, N. and Greenstein, D. (1998). Managing Digital Collections: AHDS
    Policies, Standards and Practices. Consultation Draft. December 1998.
    <http://www.ahds.ac.uk/policies.htm>

    Section 2.9.2 Technical Standards, provides a summary of preferred formats
    recommended by AHDS service providers. Further details are available in
    individual Guides to Good Practice.

2. DLM Forum. (1997). Guidelines on Best Practice for Using Electronic Information.
    <http://europa.eu.int/ISPO/dlm/documents/gdlines.pdf>

    Chapter 5, Short and long-term preservation of electronic information, offers
    advice on data storage media (including advice on storage conditions) and file
    formats. The general advice is "Best practice is to decide on a common set of
    standards from the outset to make it easier to circulate information. Preferably
    the same formats should be used for both short-term and long-term preservation".

Both storage media and file formats are grouped into families, with examples of the major types in each.

3. Public Record Office (Victoria). Standard for the Management of Electronic Records. PROS 99/007. Version 1.0 April 2000.
   <http://www.pro.vic.gov.au/gservice/standard/pros9907.htm>

   Designed for the Victorian public sector records (but with much that is applicable at a more global level) the standard provides three specifications which provide:
   1) technical detail about the long-term preservation of electronic records;
   2) the requirements for records management systems which maintain electronic records; and
   3) the metadata required for the proper management and retention of electronic records.

4. TASI. Framework: Data Capture and Creation.
   <http://www.tasi.ac.uk/framework/framework.html>
   Includes general advice on selecting file formats for images.

Costs

• Specific Case Studies of Digitisation Projects

1. Internet Library of Early Journals (ILEJ). (1999).
   <http://www.bodley.ox.ac.uk/ilej>

   This eLib project involved the universities of Birmingham, Leeds, Manchester, and Oxford and investigated the feasibility of digitising substantial runs of selected 18th and 19th century British journals. The final report of the project makes a number of observations and recommendations. The chapter on costs indicates an estimated cost of £4.21 per indexed page image accessible on the Internet but notes that "this estimate of expenditure does not take into account the contribution of the IT and library infrastructure of the four institutions". Archiving costs have been estimated at £20 per Gb per annum, totalling around £2,400 p.a. for the ILEJ project. The long-term future and funding of this was still unclear in June 2000.

2. Lee, S. (1999). Scoping the Future of the University of Oxford's Digital Library Collections: Final Report.
   <http://www.Bodley.ox.ac.uk/scoping/report.html>

   Appendix E, Digitization Method, includes examples of costs established from projects, including JIDI, BUILDER, and the Wilfred Owen project. It also cites examples of the cost-effectiveness of outsourcing.

• General guidance on estimating costs of creating digital surrogates

3. Puglia, S. (1999). 'The Costs of Digital Imaging Projects'. RLG DigiNews 3(5) October 15 1999.
   <http://www.rlg.ac.uk/preserv/diginews/diginews3-5.html>

   Averages data from a number of individual projects and estimates that for production costs, approximately one-third are for digital conversion, slightly less than one-third are for metadata creation, slightly more than one-third are for other activities, such as administration and quality control. This article also makes the important point that long-term maintenance of the digital images and associated metadata is often not considered as part of project costs but needs to be planned for. However, the article also notes that there are few models for estimating these and they vary considerably.

4. Tanner, S. and Lomax-Smith, J. (1999). 'How Much Does It Really Cost? Paper for DRH '99 Conference.
<http://heds.herts.ac.uk/resources/papers/drh99.pdf>

This article provides general advice on project management and includes a matrix of potential cost factors which can be used to estimate the costs of a digitisation project.

• Comparative Costs of Digitisation, Microform and Paper

5. Kingma, B. (1999). The Economics of Digital Access: the Early Canadiana Online Project.
<http://www.canadiana.org/eco/english/kingma.pdf>

This is an extremely detailed but highly specific investigation into the comparative costs of digital, print and microfiche access for the early Canadiana online project. The purpose of the project was "to lay the groundwork for the costing and creation of a Canadian digital collection and database to be made available on the Internet." This report effectively amounts to a detailed business case for making rare collections available via the Internet. It concludes that the cost of digital information is lower on a cost per library or per patron basis so long as a sufficient number of libraries are interested in subscribing to the database.

• Costs of maintaining digital archives

These sources are quite different from the costs referred to above which indicate the cost of creating digital surrogates. The costs here relate to maintaining digital materials, whether those materials consist of the output of digitising analogue originals (digital surrogates), or whether they are materials which are "born digital".

In a sense they are the most critical of all as they amount to largely recurrent costs which will need to be planned and budgeted for. For example, while an organisation might receive one-off funding from an external source for the purposes of creating a digital surrogate, the costs of maintaining the surrogate over time will need to be borne by the host institution. Depending on the significance of the digital resource, they may well need to be factored into an organisational budget indefinitely. Institutions which are creating digital surrogates and also taking responsibility for maintaining them are in a better position, as they can ensure that steps are taken at the outset which will minimise future maintenance costs and protect the initial investment. Those who are acquiring digital resources will have less control and will find it more difficult to predict costs reliably over time.

As indicated by Puglia (see above Puglia, 1999), these costs are the most difficult to find models for and can vary. The following references are based on practical experience. Hendley extrapolates a generic cost model based on different categories of digital objects (see below Hendley, 1998).

6. Ashley, K. (1999). 'Digital Archive Costs: Facts and Fallacies.' DLM Forum '99. <http://europa.eu.int/ISPO/dlm/fulltext/full_ash_en.htm>

    Two extremes of models are explored from the "basic safety deposit" model, in which data are deposited, but not expected to be accessed other than by the depositor, to a more comprehensive service. The latter is assumed to be the most common model and nine potential service elements are identified to provide assistance to archives in evaluating their major cost influences. There is also an indication of what factors will increase costs. In general, the simpler it is to acquire material (for example, one large file v many small ones, a restricted number of file formats v no control over deposited material, etc.), the easier it will be to reduce costs. The experience of the University of London Computing Centre is that staff account for 70% of total costs and the next greatest cost is capital and maintenance costs for hardware and software associated with access (as opposed to data preservation).

7. Dollar, Charles. (1999). Authentic Electronic Records: Strategies for Long-Term Access. Chicago: Cohasset Associates. (ISBN 0-9700640-0-4) Costs. Appendix 4

8. Hendley, T. (1998). Comparison of Methods and Costs of Digital Preservation. British Library Research and Innovation Report 109. London: the British Library. <http://www.ukoln.ac.uk/services/elib/papers/tavistock/hendley/hendley.html>

    One of seven JISC/NPO commissioned reports which investigated various aspects of digital preservation. The terms of reference for this report were:

*   To draw up a matrix of data types and categories of digital resources.
*   To draw up a decision model for assessing the agreed categories of digital resources to determine the most appropriate method of long-term preservation.
*   To draw up a cost model for comparing the costs of the preferred methods of preservation for each category of digital resource.

    Chapter 5 describes a cost model using the seven modules proposed by Beagrie and Greenstein (data creation; data selection and evaluation; data management; resource disclosure; data use; data preservation; rights management). These are first analysed to identify generic cost elements and then applied in more detail to four categories of digital resources (data sets; structured texts; office documents; visual images).

9. Russell, K. and Weinberger, E. (2000). Cost Elements of Digital Preservation. Draft 31 May 2000. <http://www.leeds.ac.uk/cedars/documents/CIW03.htm>

    Drawing on experience gained in the Cedars project, the paper discusses eight cost elements involved in preserving digital objects.

Training – creating/managing digital resources

The following organisations offer access to a range of training courses and workshops relating to creating and managing digital resources either organised themselves and/or linking to others.

1. Arts and Humanities Data Service.
    Website: <http://ahds.ac.uk>

2. Higher Education Digitisation Service (HEDS)
    Website: <http://heds.herts.ac.uk>

3. Humanities Advanced Technology and Information Institute (HATII),
    University of Glasgow.
    Website: <http://www.hatii.arts.gla.ac.uk>

4. Humanities Computing Unit, University of Oxford.
    Website: <http://www.hcu.ox.ac.uk>

5. Technical Advisory Service (TASI)
    Website: <http://www.tasi.ac.uk>

Training – electronic records management

6. Public Record Office
    Website: <http://www.pro.gov.uk/recordsmanagement>
    Training and consultancy services.

4.2 Acquisition and Appraisal, Retention and Review

4.2.1 Appraisal and Selection

In a digital environment, decisions taken at creation and selection have significant implications for preservation. The link between access and preservation is far more explicit than for paper and other traditional materials, as access to a digital resource can be lost within a relatively brief period of time if active steps are not taken to maintain (i.e. preserve) it from the beginning. As the Decision Tree below indicates, if it is neither feasible nor desirable to preserve a digital resource across various changes in technology, then its acquisition should be re-evaluated. While many of the same principles from the traditional preservation environment can usefully be applied, policies and procedures will need to be adapted to the digital environment. In a print environment, the decision to select, and the decision to preserve, can be taken quite separately and within a timeframe which may span several decades. The brief period during which digital resources will inevitably become inaccessible means that it makes sense to make decisions about selection and preservation simultaneously.

While this may mean that greater rigour is required in selecting digital resources than for printed or other analogue material, it will avoid costs which will otherwise occur further down the track as retrospective preservation of digital resources is not recommended. In these cases, as the digital resources become inaccessible, the only pragmatic option is likely to be to de-select, an activity which is in any case not without cost and one which should preferably occur as a result of a conscious decision based on sound policies, rather than by default.

Accurate documentation is also crucial in the digital environment. This will provide not only essential details for managing the resource over time but also information on context without which there may be little point in preserving the digital object itself even if it is technically feasible to do so. In the following Decision Tree, it is suggested that acquisition be re-evaluated if documentation is inadequate.

In the case of networked digital resources, where providing access to a resource does not necessarily require bringing the resource physically into a collection, the concept of acquisition is quite different from traditional collections. There are a range of options available to provide access or to build 'virtual collections'. For example, making copies/mirrors for access, providing a hyper link to a resource, online catalogues and finding aids.

Whereas acquiring a resource in the non-networked environment usually implies keeping it, in the networked digital environment, it is possible

Organisational Activities

to provide access to a resource without undertaking any preservation commitment either short or long-term. A number of institutions have adopted a selection policy based on levels of acquisition. For example, the Berkeley Digital Library sunsite[2] adopts four levels (Archived; Served; Mirrored; Linked)[3]; the AHDS[3] have articulated five levels (Archived; Served; Brokered; Linked; Finding Aids); while the National Library of Canada[4] has three levels (Archived; Served; Linked). Adapting policies to the digital environment in examples such as these is likely to be the most cost-effective means of ensuring appropriate management and continued access to the most important digital resources. In practice adopting collection levels and being explicit about preservation commitments is a crucial element of preservation policy and procedures.

In a digital environment acceptance of preservation responsibility implies significant costs. On the other hand, failing to consider short and long-term access at selection is likely to mean loss of the resource shortly after acquisition. In some cases (potentially many cases for electronic publications), an institution may be reluctant to take primary preservation responsibility for materials it acquires if it feels that interest in its preservation is so widely shared that it would constitute an unfair burden on their own institution. This emphasises the need for collaboration between institutions and the need to establish equitable agreements for shared efforts where necessary. The following decision tree for appraisal and selection is based on the assumption that the resource has not yet been acquired and indicates a number of points at which cost implications will need to be taken into account before the decision to proceed with acquisition. It suggests that, at these points, difficult decisions may need to be made about whether the resource justifies the costs required or whether it is preferable not to proceed with acquisition.

together with subsequent editions or withdrawn.
- Expiry or termination of a licence or data exchange agreement and withdrawal/return of a digital resource to the data supplier.
- Cost to sustain the data resource outweighs the value/benefit received.
- Deterioration in the quality service provided by a supplier or deterioration in the accessibility of content due to poor updating of indexing, imaging, or other characteristics internal to the data resource.

Within archives and records management professions the use of retention periods and schedules is well established. Records may be destroyed at the end of their retention period, retained for a further period, or transferred to an institution for long-term preservation.

In any collection environment it is important that written procedures are in place for the process of retention and review. The timescales, circumstances, and authorisation procedures for the review should be clearly stated. Depending on the institution's business environment, its users and depositors may be consulted as part of the process. Any recommendations may then be referred for approval to management and committees as appropriate to the size and significance of the resource.

Where a recommendation is made to de-accession an archived resource there should be procedures to consult with other stakeholders to determine whether transfer to another organisation should occur. In such cases the institution should agree conditions of transfer which include acceptable levels of care for the resource and access to it as appropriate for educational and research users.

Accessioned digital resources that have not been retained after review should retain their entry in any institutional catalogue with comments identifying the process undertaken and any transfer details.

4.2.3 Accessioning

Institutions should develop a range of accessioning procedures which support their preservation policies and objectives. These may include elements from the following list as appropriate to the item being accessioned:

Transfer procedures and guidelines
Most institutions will need to develop procedures and documents to support the smooth transfer of digital resources from suppliers into their collections. Figure 5 below outlines options for transfer and accessioning of file formats and storage media. Decisions on file formats and media (see **4.3**) will support and be interdependent with this process.

Organisational Activities

Figure 5
Options for Transfer and Accessioning of File Formats and Storage Media

Options	Issue	Requirements
		• Policy on storage formats. • Technology Watch on developments in storage formats. (all options)
Limit range of file formats received **Limit range of media received (most cost-effective long-term option)**	• Simplifies management and reduces overall costs. • Depositor may lack resource or expertise to comply. • Wide variety of file formats used and proprietary extensions to open standards. • Media used for transfer potentially can be used for long-term storage.	• Guidelines on preferred formats. • Degree of influence over the deposit. • Outreach and collaboration strategies to achieve desired outcomes. • Guidelines on preferred transfer media and transfer procedures.
Accept as received but convert to standard file format **Accept as received but convert to standard storage media format**	• Simplifies management and reduces longer term costs. • May not be technically feasible to convert to standard format. • It will be necessary to check that accidental loss of data has not occurred.	• Copyright permissions or statutory preservation rights. • Resources and technical expertise at host institution. • Election of preferred formats. • Documentation of native formats to allow conversion. • Integrity checks for conversion process.
Accept and store as received (least cost-effective option long-term, despite lower initial costs)	• Complicates management and increases costs of managing resources over time. • High risk option, particularly if large numbers of digital resources are being collected. • A choice of file formats may be available. That deposited may not be the most suitable for preservation. • Storage media may be of unknown quality and suitability for long-term preservation. • Formats may be obsolete or not supported within the institution.	• Clearly defined priorities for both short and long-term preservation. • Ability to address issues such as encryption, proprietary software etc. in received items. • Ability to ensure future access to information contained in the item.

Procedures to prepare data and documentation for
storage and preservation

Unique numbering
Each data resource accessioned by an institution should be allocated a
unique identifier. This number will identify the resource in the Institution's
catalogue and be used to locate or identify physical media and documentation.
In the event of a resource being de-accessioned for any reason, this unique
number should not be re-allocated.

Preferred marking and labelling
At a minimum all physical media and hard copy documentation should be
marked with the unique number allocated to the resource, and any additional
information required by the institution easily to identify content and formats.

Handling guidelines
Handling guidelines for accessioning staff should be developed reflecting
storage and preservation staff advice on best practice for different media
(see **Chapter 5**).

Validation
Validation checks should be carried out by the institution on the transfer
media, content and structure of deposited data resources, and on any
accompanying documentation. Validation procedures may be adapted in the
light of the volumes of material and resources available in the acquisitions
section. It may be possible to automate some of the validation procedures
but others can only be undertaken manually. Such checks may include:
- Scanning for computer viruses.
- Checking media and files can be read.
- Checking completeness and accuracy of paper based or digital
  documentation.
- Checking description and intellectual content of the resource.
- Checking structure and formatting of the resource.
- Procedures for documenting validation checks and any discrepancies
  encountered.
- Procedures for checking and if possible resolving discrepancies with the
  supplier.

Re-formatting file formats
Where the file formats used to transfer the resource are unsuitable for
long-term preservation, the Institution may re-format the resource onto
its preferred file formats. In addition to archive formats, versions in other
formats suitable for delivery to users may also be produced from the
original (see **4.3**).

Re-formatting storage media

Where the storage media used to transfer the resource are unsuitable for long-term preservation, the Institution may re-format the resource onto its preferred media (see **4.3**).

Copying

Multiple backup copies of an item may be generated during accessioning as part of institutions' storage and preservation policy and to enable disaster recovery procedures (see **4.3**).

Security

System and physical security policies and procedures should be in place to ensure the care and integrity of items during accessioning. These should be developed from and reflect the institutional policies and procedures on security (see **4.3**).

4.2.4 Cataloguing and Documentation Procedures

Cataloguing

Each institution normally identifies its own minimum standard of information required for catalogued items in the collection. Each institution can also identify its preferred levels of cataloguing information and documentation for acquisitions and may notify and encourage suppliers or depositors to supply this information through the deposit or acquisition process. Staff review and revise supplied documentation to ensure it conforms to institutional guidelines and they generate catalogue records for deposited data incorporating cataloguing and documentation standards to ensure that information about those items can be made available to users through appropriate catalogues. In many cases the contextual information for resources will be crucial to their future use and this aspect of documentation should not be overlooked.

The level of cataloguing and documentation accompanying or subsequently added to an item, and any limitations these may impose can be documented for the benefit of future users. Where data resources are managed by third parties but made available via an institution, documentation may be supplied by the third party in an agreed form which conforms to institution guidelines or in the supplier's native format.

Retrospective documentation or catalogue enhancement

Where a need for enhanced access exists, an Institution may undertake to enhance documentation and cataloguing information to a higher standard to meet new requirements. Retrospective documentation or catalogue enhancement should also occur when the validating or audit of the documentation and cataloguing for a resource shows this to be below a minimum acceptable standard.

Edition and version control

Procedures for updating and edition control of any dynamic data resources accessioned (e.g. annual snapshots of databases which are regularly being updated) or for version control of accessioned items where appropriate (e.g. items accessioned in different formats or for which different formats for preservation and access had been generated.)

Cataloguing and documentation standards

Data documentation is essential in order effectively to exchange information and documents between platforms and individuals. At a minimum, it should provide information about an item's provenance and administrative history (including any data processing involved since its creation), contents, structure, and about the terms and conditions attached to its subsequent management and use.

It should be sufficiently detailed to support:
- Resource discovery (e.g. the location of a resource which is at least briefly described along with many other resources).
- Resource evaluation (e.g. the process by which a user determines whether s/he requires access to that resource).
- Resource ordering (e.g. that information which instructs a user about the terms and conditions attached to a resource and the processes or other means by which access to that resource may be acquired).
- Resource use (e.g. that information which may be required by a user in order to access the resource's information content).
- Resource management (e.g. administrative information essential to a resource's management and preservation as part of a broader collection and including information about location, version control, etc).

Processing times

Ideally targets should be set and monitored for the maximum time between acquisition and cataloguing to prevent backlogs of unprocessed and potentially at risk materials developing during the accessioning process.

Summary of recommendations

Transfer procedures
- Provide documentation to guide and support transfer of digital resources from suppliers.
- Decide how your transfer procedures can best be developed to support your storage and preservation policies.

Procedures to prepare data and documentation for storage and preservation

- Unique numbering of each item accessioned.
- Marking and labelling procedures.
- Handling guidelines for different media.
- Validation procedures to check media, content, and structure.
- Re-formatting of file or storage media formats according to agreed guidelines.
- Generating multiple copies of an item as part of an institution's storage and preservation policy.
- System and physical security policy and procedures for items during accessioning.

Procedures for cataloguing and documentation

- A minimum standard of information required for cataloguing.
- Guidelines for retrospective documentation or catalogue enhancement.
- Procedures for updating, and managing versions or editions of an item.
- Procedures to update collection management databases.
- Selection of cataloguing and documentation standard.
- Targets for accessioning tasks and timescales for their completion.

References

1. See Ross, S. and Gow, A. (1999). Digital Archaeology: Rescuing Neglected and Damaged Data Resources. p. 29.
   <http://www.hatii.arts.gla.ac.uk/Projects/BrLibrary/rosgowrt.pdf>

2. Berkeley Digital Library Sunsite.
   <http://sunsite.berkeley.edu/Admin/collection.html>

3. National Library of Canada. (1998). Networked Electronic Publications: Policy and Guidelines. p. 7-8. Online. Available:
   <http://www.nlc-bnc.ca/9/8/index-e.html>

Organisational Activities

Exemplars and Further Reading

1. Reference Model for an Open Archival Information System (OAIS) Draft
    Recommendation for Space Data System Standard. May 1999.
    <http://www.ccsds.org/RP9905/RP9905.html>

    The OAIS Reference Model provides a useful overview of the "ingest" process
    and a high-level process model relevant to most institutions.

2. Beagrie, N and Greenstein, D. (1998). Managing Digital Collections: AHDS
    Policies, Standards and Practices. Consultation Draft. December 1998.
    <http://www.ahds.ac.uk/policies.htm>

    Provides a summary of preferred formats recommended by AHDS service
    providers, and accessioning and transfer procedures use by the AHDS. It also
    includes two detailed case studies of accessioning in the History Data Service
    and the Oxford Text Archive.

4. National Archive of New Zealand. (1998). Appraisal Standard, Standard for the
    Appraisal of Public Records and Archives. Wellington, 1998.
    <http://www.archives.govt.nz/statutory_regulatory/reviews/appraisal_service/
    options_paper.html>

5. Public Record Office (UK). (1999). Electronic Records from Office
    Systems Project (EROS). Series of guides on management, appraisal and
    preservation of electronic records in government. Kew, Surrey, 1999.
    <http://www.pro.gov.uk/recordsmanagement/eros/default.htm>

4.3   Storage and Preservation

Maintaining access to digital resources over the long-term involves inter-dependent strategies for preservation in the short to medium term based on safeguarding storage media, content and documentation, and computer software and hardware; and strategies for long-term preservation to address the issues of software and hardware obsolescence. This section is therefore divided into two parts: the first dealing with storage and maintenance of digital resources; and the second with strategies for their long-term preservation.

A preservation strategy for digital resources is most effective if it addresses the full life-cycle of the resource allowing the greatest efficiencies between data creation, preservation and use. This section should therefore be read in conjunction with related sections and chapters particularly the other sections of this chapter **4** and chapter **5**.

Storage of digital resources supports both access and preservation. Depending on the needs of the organisation and the media, it may be necessary to create both preservation and access copies and to have strategies for each. We have used the term "digital preservation" in this handbook to define all the activities employed to ensure continued access to digital resources which have retained properties of authenticity, integrity and functionality. The term "archiving" can be substituted for preservation provided this definition remains. Archiving is usually interpreted within the computing industry simply to indicate that something has been stored and is no longer immediately accessible. The richer interpretation used here means that there will need to be more thought and preparation given to what resources are stored, how they are maintained and subsequently accessed and by whom.

There is no single definitive solution which can be applied for the preservation of any digital resource. However, an approach which is based on good management practices commenced as early as possible in the lifecycle of a resource, will safeguard the initial investment and facilitate authorised access at least for the short to medium term. Preventive preservation is as crucial a strategy in preservation programmes for digital resources as it is for non-digital material and good storage practice plays a major role in both. Key initial decisions needing to be made by institutions taking responsibility for short- or long-term preservation of digital resources will be:

1) Whether storage and/or preservation will be undertaken by the host institution or under contract to a trusted third party (see **3.3** for discussion of issues relating to whether or not to outsource);

2) Which resources justify preservation and for what period of time.

The assumption in 2) is that not all resources can or need to be preserved forever, some will not need to be preserved at all, others will need to be preserved only for a defined period of time, a relatively small sub-set will need to be preserved indefinitely. Making this decision as early as possible will help to conserve resources for the most valuable digital assets.

This section deals with the range of strategies and approaches which will help to ensure important digital resources do not become inaccessible prematurely. Many constitute a relatively modest investment compared to the initial costs of creating the resource, which are often substantial. They can also represent significant cost savings longer term. In any event, failure to commit resources to managing digital resources throughout their lifecycle will inevitably result in their loss and/or costly restoration so investment in strategies to prevent this is eminently justified.

4.3.1 Storage and Maintenance

Storage media and file formats

General advice on storage media and file formats is provided in **chapter 5**. Policy and selection of storage media and file formats will have implications for institutional strategies such as outreach and development of standards and best practice guidelines (see **3.2** and **3.6**) and for accessioning (see **4.2**). Decisions will need to be made during accessioning on whether to store resources as received or to reformat. A table outlining options, issues and requirements to assist with this decision process is provided in **4.2.3**.

Management of media and systems

Media refreshing and reformatting
Rationale
An essential management component for all digital media to avoid media degradation and to facilitate longer term preservation strategies.
Requirements
- Needs to be part of an ongoing regime so appropriate resources are required.
- Reformat data resources onto selected archival media if necessary.
- Write archive copies with different software to protect data against corruption from malfunctioning or virus- or bug-ridden software.
- Write archive to comparable magnetic media purchased from different suppliers to guard against faults introduced by the media's suppliers into their products or into batches of their products.
- Refresh or transfer archive copies to new media at specified times. This should take place:
  - within the minimum time specified by the supplier for the media's viability

under prevailing environmental conditions;

- when new storage devices are installed;
- when an audit discloses significant temporary or read "errors" in a data resource.
- Employ quality control procedure such as bit/byte or other checksum comparisons with originals to ensure the authenticity and integrity of items after media refreshing.
- Document actions taken when data resources are copied.
- Retain copies of the digital resource in its original format whenever some information or presentation of the resource may be lost or modified in re-formatting.

Disaster recovery planning

Rationale

The development and use of a disaster recovery plan based on sound principles, endorsed by senior management, and able to be activated by trained staff will greatly reduce the severity of the impact of disasters and incidents.

"The assumption is that with good disaster planning data recovery will be, under most circumstances, unnecessary. The problem is that while attention has been paid to disaster planning and the identification of good recovery procedures the effectiveness of these tend to depend upon pre-disaster effort. This effort often never takes place."[1]

Requirements

- Develop counter disaster plan to operate in the event of natural or man-made disasters. One model is the Disaster Recovery Procedures developed by the Data Archive, copied below, with the permission of the Data Archive.
- Ensure all relevant staff are trained in counter disaster procedures.
- Create archive copies of data resources at the time of their transfer to the institution.
- Store archive copies on industry standard digital tape or on other approved contemporary media.
- Store archive copies on and off site. Off-site copies should be stored at a safe distance from on-site copies to ensure they are unaffected by any natural or man-made disaster affecting the on-site copies.

Case study – disaster recovery procedures – UK Data Archive, University of Essex

The mission of the UK Data Archive is to support high quality research, teaching and learning in the social sciences and humanities; by acquiring, developing and managing data and related digital resources. It has over 4000 mainstream digital datasets or studies, comprising over 151,000 individual files.

The digital storage system at the Data Archive is based on a Hierarchical Storage Management System (HSM) where the files appear to be local to the user but are mainly based on tape. As each file is requested it is either brought back from the disk cache on the system or automatically "restored" from the required tape. Any subsequent requests for that file are returned from disk cache.

Disaster recovery at the Data Archive is based around the resilience provided by creating multiple copies of the data and specified recovery procedures. Each file from any dataset has at least four copies and these are as follows:

Main copy This copy is held on the main area on the HSM file system.

Shadow copy At least one shadow copy is made. As files are updated, they are "shadowed" onto a separate tape in the main system. Multiple versions of these files are kept to allow staff to go back to a previous version of a file.

CD-ROM copy A CD-ROM is created for each dataset as part of the preservation procedure. This allows staff to access an alternate local source in the case of downtime of the main system and serves as an alternative long-term storage media. For each study all of the files are compressed and stored as a single zip file and written on to a CD-ROM. Subsequent updates to this study are created as complete zip files xxxx_2.zip and appended to the existing CD-ROM for that study.

Off-site near-line copy An off-site, near-line copy is kept in case of a major disaster at Essex. Due to restrictions of small file sizes on these systems, these are kept in the form of a range of datasets, which have been grouped together, compressed and encrypted.

Disasters can occur in different forms and at varying levels. The Data Archive has in place a range of recovery measures designed to meet any conceivable disaster.

- **Corrupt file**
  A file is supplied with corrupt information that is not detected through Data Processing
  Solution
  A. The file is re-requested from the supplier.
  B. Older version(s) of the file are retrieved from the shadow area and are either supplied back to the depositor or used to replace the corrupt file.

- **Unreadable file**
  A single file is unreadable from the media due to a bad block on a tape
  Solution
  A. The tape is checked to make certain that this is an isolated problem. If it is found to affect the complete tape the corrupt media disaster recovery procedure is activated.
  B. If the problem is isolated then the problematic file is recreated from the shadow area.

- **Corrupt media**
  In this case a complete tape is damaged or cannot be reliably read.
  Solution
  A. If the tape was full and was set as read only and a refreshed tape was available then that could be copied to regenerate a new tape.
  B. If no retired refreshed media was available then a new tape could be created by retrieving the files from the shadow area, which are held on separate tapes. This process would require about 8 hours downtime of the HSM system. This process has been successfully used after a tape was damaged in the library due to a firmware fault on the DLT.

- **Corrupt shadow area as well as main area**
  In this situation both the main and shadow areas cannot be read, nor any of the refreshed tapes.
  Solution
  This is very unlikely due to the number of checks that are made but in the event, the study or data would be re-created from the read-only CD-ROM copy. A CD-ROM copy is generated when the data is placed onto the preservation system and so would be up to date.

- **Complete loss of data at the University of Essex**
  In this scenario, all of the data held at the University of Essex are unreadable and all of the systems are damaged beyond repair. (Major disaster.)
  Solution
  The main HSM systems would be built and data would be retrieved from the off-site holdings at ULCC.

Source: The Data Archive. Systems and Preservation Procedures(1999 unpublished) reproduced with the kind permission of the Data Archive.

Environmental conditions

Rationale

Appropriate environmental conditions will increase the longevity of digital storage media and help prevent accidental damage to a data resource or its documentation.

Requirement

- Follow relevant guidance on environmental conditions for storage media in BS 4783.

  Note: Most experts agree that large fluctuations in temperature and humidity are more damaging than having slightly higher than ideal temperature and Relative Humidity (RH). See, for example Van Bogart (1995)[2].

The following figure summarises British Standard 4783.

Figure 6

Summary of Environmental Conditions Recommended in BS 4783 for Data Storage Media

Device	Operating	Non-Operating	Long term storage
Magnetic tape cassettes 12.7mm	18 to 24°C 45 to 55% RH	5 to 32°C 5 to 80% RH	18 to 22°C 35 to 45% RH
Magnetic tape cartridges	10 to 45°C 20 to 80% RH	5 to 45°C 20 to 80% RH	18 to 22°C 35 to 45% RH
Magnetic tape 4 & 8mm helical scan	5 to 45°C 20 to 80% RH	5 to 45°C 20 to 80% RH	5 to 32°C 20 to 60% RH
CD-ROM	10 to 50°C 10 to 80% RH	-10 to 50°C 5 to 90% RH	18 to 22°C 35 to 45% RH

Extracts from BS 4783 reproduced with the permission of the British Standards Institution under licence number 2001/SK0280

- Establish guidance and procedures for acclimatising magnetic tape if moving between significant variations in temperature (e.g. tapes moving from very cold external conditions should not be used before being acclimatised to warmer internal conditions).
- Establish procedures for monitoring environmental conditions.
- Minimise risk of damage from dust and other airborne pollutants.
- Prohibit smoking and eating in the storage area.
- Store away from direct sunlight.
- Provide additional protection in the form of enclosures for media.
- Provide storage facilities which minimise the threat from natural disasters such as fire and flood or to magnetic storage media from magnetic fields.
- Ensure any non-digital accompanying materials (e.g. codebooks, operating instructions) are also stored in appropriate environmental conditions.

Care and handling

Rationale

Appropriate care and handling will protect fragile digital media from damage.

Requirements

- Establish written guidelines and procedures based on available guidance (see **Further Reading** to this section and **chapter 5**).

Audit

Rationale

There needs to be assurance that the resource has not been inadvertently or deliberately changed following refreshment and/or migration procedures and to check the readability and integrity of the data over time.

Requirements

- Check media periodically for their readability. Such checking may be conducted automatically in mass storage systems according to parameters set by system operators.
- Check the integrity of data files periodically using checksum procedures. Such procedures may be implemented automatically in mass storage systems according to parameters set by system operators.
- Employ appropriate security systems and procedures to protect the authenticity of items in your holdings (see **Security** below).

Security

Rationale

Rigorous security procedures will a) ensure compliance with any legal and regulatory requirements; b) protect digital resources from inadvertent or deliberate changes; c) provide an audit trail to satisfy accountability requirements; d) act as a deterrent to potential internal security breaches; e) protect the authenticity of digital resources; f) safeguard against theft or loss.

It is important to note that not all digital resources will require identical levels of security. Some, for example commercial in-confidence, will require more rigorous security regimes than less sensitive material. Guidance on levels of security can be found in BS 7799 Information Security Management[3]. All personal data will need to conform with the requirements of the Data Protection Act (1998)[4].

Requirements

- Establish disaster recovery plan (see above).
- Control access to storage facilities and processing areas. Store in separate, preferably lockable area.
- Ensure no unauthorised access.
- Design audit features into mass storage systems and computerised physical access controls. Undertake regular random checks if automated audits are not feasible.

- Establish procedures to ensure no deliberate or inadvertent changes can take place.
- Ensure all legal requirements are met.
- Establish procedures for ensuring authenticity.
- Use passwords and user ids, and other network security procedures.
- Define system and area access privileges for staff.
- Assign specific staff responsibilities for data security and storage facilities.

Management of computer storage

Rationale

Unlike storage space for physical collections, computer storage is both reducing in cost and increasing in capacity all the time. Costs for processor capacity and storage media are expected to continue to drop (halving every 18 months at least according to Moore's Law) for several years to come[5]. However while storage is much less of a problem than it was, it conforms to good practice to establish policies and procedures which clarify what digital resources need to be accessible online, nearline or offline. Digital resources can be generated relatively easily, and the prospects for storage space to become cluttered with several versions of documents and other less valuable digital resources are quite high. It makes sense to establish when certain categories of resources may be automatically removed from online storage after a defined period of time, when others will be re-assessed, and which resources will be considered to be sacrosanct.

These decisions will need to be well documented and understood by all stakeholders within the institution.

Requirements

- Policies for maintaining documents on central file server (See **Exemplars and Further Reading**, page 112, Storage and Maintenance, Oxford University Policy on Computer Archiving Services).
- Strategies for migrating to larger file server before full capacity is reached.
- Policies to identify which digital resources should be stored online.
- Retention policies to determine at what stage (if ever) online storage of digital resources will be re-assessed (see also **4.2**).

4.3.2 Preservation Strategies

This section is divided into primary preservation strategies and secondary preservation strategies. Primary preservation strategies as defined here are those which might be selected by an archiving repository for medium to long-term preservation of digital materials for which they have accepted preservation responsibility. Secondary preservation strategies are those which might be employed in the short to medium term either by the repository with long-term preservation responsibility and/or by those with a more transient interest in the materials. Chronologically, secondary strategies may precede primary strategies. Some secondary strategies may substantially defer the need for, or alternatively greatly strengthen, primary preservation strategies so describing them as secondary strategies does not necessarily imply their inferiority. Two strategies dominate current options for preserving digital resources long-term, these are migration and emulation. Both have champions and detractors, both have acknowledged difficulties. The need for both may also be deferred and/or simplified if appropriate preventive preservation procedures such as storage and maintenance (see **4.3.1**) and selected secondary preservation strategies, have been used.

The other potential long-term strategy, converting to an analogue preservation format, differs from the other strategies in two important ways:

1. It can only sensibly be considered for a relatively small category of digital resources and is patently inappropriate for the increasing numbers of more complex digital resources being created.
2. By its nature, it loses the digital characteristics of the resources it converts and is therefore a preservation strategy for some digital resources, as opposed to a digital preservation strategy, where the essential aim is to retain the digital characteristics of the resource. The latter should be preferred.

Another option represented here as a secondary strategy is digital archaeology (secondary strategy 7). This is not precisely a preservation strategy at all but rather when the absence of preservation strategies has left valuable resources inaccessible.

It should be emphasised that employing a judicious mix of secondary strategies 1-5 combined with responsible storage and maintenance decisions in **4.2** has the potential significantly to reduce both risks of losing access to digital resources in the short-term and costs of preserving access to them in the long-term.

Primary preservation strategies

Preservation strategies selected by archiving repositories with long-term preservation responsibility for the digital materials in their care. It should be noted that discussion of costs in this context is of necessity based on educated assumptions as opposed to empirical evidence gathered over a very long timeframe. Cost models for complex digital materials particularly those of recent origin are still at the research stage at the time of writing.

Migration

Description

A means of overcoming technological obsolescence by transferring digital resources from one hardware/software generation to the next. The purpose of migration is to preserve the intellectual content of digital objects and to retain the ability for clients to retrieve, display, and otherwise use them in the face of constantly changing technology. Migration differs from the refreshing of storage media in that it is not always possible to make an exact digital copy or replicate original features and appearance and still maintain the compatibility of the resource with the new generation of technology.

(Note: There are differing degrees of migration, ranging from relatively straightforward conversion to a major paradigm shift. Obviously the latter category will be most relevant to the disadvantages outlined below. It should also be noted that by using the secondary preservation strategy of standards, it may be possible to delay the need for migration).

Advantages
- Procedures for simple migration are well established.
- Is currently the preferred strategy for most digital archives.
- May become simpler as technology advances and range of platforms diminishes.
- A recent CLIR publication has produced a risk assessment tool to assist decision-making[6].

Disadvantages
- Cost – requires special program to be written for complex migrations.
- Can be time-consuming and complex.
- Likely to lose some functionality and look and feel of original.
- May compromise the integrity of the originals unless stringent quality control procedures to ensure authenticity are in place.
- More complex digital resources may be migrated with significant loss of functionality.
- Needs to occur at regular intervals throughout the life of the resource. See Rothenberg[7] for more detailed discussion of what he considers to be major drawbacks to migration as a digital preservation strategy.

Requirements
- Written policies and guidelines, including selection policy for materials to be migrated.
- Quality control procedures.
- Rigorous documentation of migration procedure.
- Preservation metadata and documentation (see **4.4**).
- Migrate data whenever there is a software upgrade or a new software application is installed.
- Ensure the migration results in little or no loss in content or context.
- Employ strict quality control procedures that may include testing the migration programme with a sample of records or bit/byte or checksum comparisons of migrated and original data.
- Retain copies of the digital resource in its original format whenever some information or presentation of the resource may be lost or modified in migration.

Related strategies
- Storage and maintenance.
- Backwards compatibility.
- Permanent identifier.
- Validation procedures.
- Conversion to standard formats.

Emulation
Description
A means of overcoming technological obsolescence of hardware and software by developing techniques for imitating obsolete systems on future generations of computers.

Advantages
- Recreates the functionality, look and feel of the original.
- Avoids repeated costs associated with migration (though see also disadvantages below).
- May offer the best prospects for more complex digital resources.

Disadvantages
- Is still in the research stage and requires further practical testing (see CAMiLEON project[8] and Rothenberg[7, 9]. See also Bearman[10] (1999) for a critique of emulation as a viable preservation strategy).
- May only be able to emulate part of the functionality, look and feel of the original.
- Is likely to be very costly unless it has economies of scale. New emulators need to be built for major computer paradigm shifts; it is possible that these costs may even exceed the savings of repeated migration costs.
- Software copyright issues need to be addressed and may be extremely complex.
- There must be rigorous documentation of hardware and software requirements. These have rarely been documented to this level of detail in the past and would require concerted effort and resources.

Requirements
- Appropriate storage and maintenance procedures (see **4.3.1**).
- Written policies and guidelines.
- Preservation metadata (see **4.4**).
- Detailed documentation on hardware and software specifications.

Related strategies
- Storage and maintenance.
- Encapsulation.
- Permanent identifiers

Secondary preservation strategies

Secondary preservation strategies are those which might be selected either by the archiving repository with long-term responsibility for the preservation of digital materials and/or by those with a more transient interest in the digital materials they have created and/or acquired. A judicious combination of secondary strategies and appropriate storage and maintenance (see **4.3.1**) can be a cost-effective means of ensuring continued access to digital materials for as long as they are needed, either deferring or in some cases, even avoiding, the need for primary preservation strategies.

Technology preservation

Description

A means of overcoming technological obsolescence by retaining the hardware and software used to access the digital resource. It should be noted that the current definition of this strategy involves individual institutions needing to maintain both hardware and software for all materials they create and/or acquire. A variation of this strategy has been suggested which involves the setting up of a facility offering documentation for hardware and software and file format specification[11,12]. If these recommendations were implemented, this variation on the technology preservation strategy could become a much more feasible proposition and provide valuable support for genuinely long-term emulation or migration strategies.

Advantages
* Storage retains the functionality, look and feel of the original.
* Storage delays the time when other preservation strategies are required.
* Storage may be the most practical interim strategy for complex digital resources.

Disadvantages
* Can only be used as a short- to medium-term strategy. Is not viable long-term as defined here.
* Technical support will inevitably disappear within a relatively short timeframe.
* Facilitating access will become increasingly problematic over time.

Requirements
* Policies and guidelines regarding access.
* Documentation of hardware and software maintained.
* Metadata required to maintain the hardware and software.

Related strategies
* Storage and maintenance.
* Conversion to standard formats.
* Backwards compatibility.
* Adherence to standards.

Adherence to standards

Description

Adhering to stable and widely adopted open standards when creating and archiving digital resources. These are not tied to specific hardware/software platforms and thus can defer inaccessibility of digital resource due to technological obsolescence. Can either be self-imposed by institutions creating digital resources, or imposed by agencies receiving digital resources (see also **3.6** and chapter **5**).

Advantages

- Using stable open standards will delay the time when more costly strategies are needed.
- Using stable standards will reduce the complexity, and therefore costs, of longer-term preservation strategies.
- Can simplify migration and achieve economies of scale in migrating similar items.
- Can benefit creators as well as long-term preservation. Helps to distribute some of the effort over the lifecycle of resources.

Disadvantages

- Dependent on creators being able and/or willing to comply or later conversion by the archive.
- Stable standards are not available for some formats.
- Even when stable standards do exist, they are themselves subject to inevitable change as they evolve into new versions.
- Proprietary extensions are relatively common and generally not as well documented as the standard itself.

Requirements

- Knowledge of all relevant standards for all categories of digital resources acquired by the institution.
- Written guidelines on preferred and acceptable standards.
- Institutional strategies for outreach, collaboration, standards and best practice.
- Technology watch on standards activities.

Related strategies

- Adherence to standards will facilitate all other digital preservation strategies.

Backwards compatibility

Description

Being able to retain accessibility to a digital resource following upgrade to new software and/or operating systems.

Advantages

- Defers for a period the need for primary preservation strategies.
- Is being offered by increasing number of vendors.

Disadvantages

- Is not routinely offered by all vendors.
- Can only be of short- to medium-term value.
- Even when it exists it cannot be expected to last indefinitely.
- Its continued availability is dependent on market forces which are notoriously volatile. It may therefore cease to be available with little or no warning.

Related strategies

- Storage and maintenance.

Encapsulation

Description

Grouping together a digital resource and whatever is necessary to maintain access to it. This can include metadata, software viewers, and discrete files forming the digital resource.

Advantages

- Ensures all supporting information required for access is maintained as one entity.
- Can potentially overcome some of the major disadvantages of alternative strategies.
- Provides a useful means of focussing attention on what elements are needed for access.

Disadvantages

- Can produce very large files with duplication (e.g. of viewers) across the collection unless these links are maintained.
- Encapsulated software is still open to rapid technological obsolescence.

Related strategies

- Emulation

Permanent identifiers

Description

A means of locating a digital object even when its location changes. Examples are Universal Resource Names (URN's); Handles; Digital Object Identifiers (DOI's); Persistent Uniform Resource Locators (PURLs)

Advantages

- Critically important in helping to establish the authenticity of a resource.
- Provides access to a resource even if its location changes.
- Overcomes the problems caused by the impermanent nature of URLs.
- Allows interoperability between collections.

Disadvantages

- There is no single system accepted by all.
- The costs of establishing or using a resolver service.
- Is dependent on ongoing maintenance of the permanent identifier system.

Related strategies
All, except Conversion to Analogue Formats.

Converting to stable analogue format

Description
Converting certain valuable digital resources to a stable analogue medium such as permanent paper or preservation microfilm or, more recently, nickel disk readable by electron microscope. This cannot be recommended as more than a pragmatic interim strategy for a small category of digital materials, pending the development of more appropriate digital preservation strategies.

Advantages
* Is no longer vulnerable to technological obsolescence assuming preservation quality microfilm or permanent paper is used.
* Should essentially be a "once only" cost for conversion.
* Will guarantee accessibility for hundreds of years provided it is converted to an archival standard and stored in archival conditions.
* May be a pragmatic interim strategy pending the development of infrastructure for more appropriate digital preservation strategies.

Disadvantages
* Loses functionality of original digital resource.
* Can only sensibly be considered as an option for digital resources which do not utilise or require the full functionality of digital technology.
* Has already caused difficulties even when used for simple text emails[6].
* Cannot be considered for more complex digital resources where loss of functionality would at best diminish, if not destroy, the usefulness and integrity of the resource.
* Loses the advantages of digital technology, for example the convenience of use, and efficient use of space.
* Costs of conversion to archival standard and storage in archival conditions (the latter cost will be recurrent and the cumulative cost will be significant over time).

Requirements
* Policies and guidelines clearly documenting rationale for adopting strategy and category of resources it may be used for.

Related strategies
* None, this is not a digital preservation strategy but a mechanism to preserve the information content of certain digital resources.

Digital archaeology

Description
Rescuing digital resources which have become inaccessible as a result of technological obsolescence and/or media degradation. Not so much a strategy in itself as a substitute for one when digital materials have fallen outside a systematic preservation programme.

Advantages

* There are a growing number of specialist third party services offering this service.
* It has been shown to be technically possible to recover a wide range of information from damaged or obsolete media (though not necessarily in the same form).

Disadvantages

* Much more costly long-term than bona fide digital preservation strategies.
* Is unlikely to be cost-effective for anything other than the most highly valued digital resources.
* Potentially useful materials which do not justify the costs involved will be lost.
* Risk that some digital materials may not be able to be successfully rescued.
* Poor management of initial investment.

References

1. Ross, S and Gow, A. (1999). Digital Archaeology: Rescuing Neglected and Damaged Data Resources. p. 3.
<http://www.hatii.arts.gla.ac.uk/Projects/BrLibrary/rosgowrt.pdf>

2. van Bogart, J. (1995). Magnetic Tape Storage and Handling. Council on Library and Information Resources. (ISBN 1-887334-40-8)
<http://www.clir.org/pubs/reports/pub54>

3. British Standards Institute. (1999). Information Security Management (BS7799-2: 1999). Order details online: <http://www.bsi-global.com/group.xhtml>

4. Data Protection Act 1998.
<http://www.hmso.gov.uk/acts/acts1998/19980029.htm>

5. For example Arms, C. (2000). 'Keeping Memory Alive: Practices for Preserving Digital Content at the National Digital Library Program of the Library of Congress.' RLG DigiNews. Volume 4 (3). June 15 2000. p. 5.
<http://www.rlg.ac.uk/preserv/diginews/diginews4-3.html>

6. Lawrence, G.W. et al. (2000). Risk Management of Digital Information: a File Format Investigation. Council on Library and Information Resources. June 2000. (ISBN 1-887334-78-5).
< http://www.clir.org/pubs/abstract/pub93abst.html>

7. Rothenberg, J. (1999). Avoiding Technological Quicksand: Finding a Viable Technical Foundation for Digital Preservation. Council on Library and Information Resources. January 1999. (ISBN 1-887334-63-7).
<http://www.clir.org/pubs/abstract/pub77.html>

8. CAMiLEON (Creative Archiving at Michigan and Leeds; Emulating the Old and the New) Project. Available from the Cedars website:
<http://.www.leeds.ac.uk/cedars>

9. Rothenberg, J. (2000). An Experiment in Using Emulation to Preserve Digital Publications. A report commissioned by the Koninklijke Bibliotheek (KB).
<http://www.kb.nl/nedlib/results/emulationpreservationreport.pdf>

10. Bearman, D. (1999). 'Reality and Chimeras in the Preservation of Electronic Records'. D-Lib Magazine. April 1999.
<http://www.dlib.org/dlib/april99/bearman/04bearman.html>

11. Ross, S. and Gow, A. (1999). Digital Archaeology: Rescuing Neglected and Damaged Data Resources. British Library Research and Innovation Report 108. London, The British Library, 1999. p. 44.
<http://www.hatii.arts.gla.ac.uk/Projects/BrLibrary/rosgowrt.pdf>

12. Lawrence, G.W. et al. (2000). Risk Management of Digital Information: a File Format Investigation. Council on Library and Information Resources. June 2000. (ISBN 1-887334-78-5). p.15.
< http://www.clir.org/pubs/abstract/pub93abst.html>

13. A striking example of the potential pitfalls of reliance of converting email to paper can be found in the PROFS case involving the National Archives and Records Administration in the USA.
<http://www.cpsr.org/cpsr/foia/PROFS_CASE/profs.html>

Exemplars and Further Reading

General overviews and guidance

1. Arms, C. (2000). 'Keeping Memory Alive: Practices for Preserving Digital Content at the National Digital Library Program of the Library of Congress'. RLG DigiNews: Volume 4 (3). June 15 2000. <http://www.rlg.ac.uk/preserv/diginews4-3.html>

2. Dollar, C. (1999). Authentic Electronic Records: Strategies for Long-Term Access. Chicago: Cohasset Associates. (ISBN 0-9700640-0-4).

3. AHDS: Guides to Good Practice <http://www.ahds.ac.uk/guides.htm>

    Titles linked in June 2001:
    Archiving Aerial Photography and Remote Sensing Data;
    Excavation and Fieldwork Archiving;
    GIS (Geographic Information Systems);
    Digitising History: a Guide to Creating Digital Resources from Historical Documents;
    Creating Digital Performance Resources;
    Creating and Documenting Electronic Texts;
    Creating Digital Resources for the Visual Arts: Standards and Good Practice.

Storage and maintenance – models and guidance

1. DLM Forum. (1997). Guidelines on Best Practice for Using Electronic Information. <http://europa.eu.int/ISPO/dlm/documents/gdlines.pdf>

2. A Digital Preservation Strategy for the PRO. November 1999.

3. National Library of Australia. First Steps in Preserving Digital Publications. 1999. <http://www.nla.gov.au/pres/epupam.html>

4. Woodyard, D. (1999). 'Practical Advice for Preserving Publications on Disk'. Presented at Information Online and Ondisc '99, Darling Harbour, Sydney, 21 January 1999. <http://www.nla.gov.au/nla/staffpaper/woodyard2.html>

5. National Library of Canada. Networked Electronic Publications: Policies and Guidelines. October 1998. <http://www.nlc-bnc.ca/9/8/index-e.html>

6. NOF-digitise Technical Standards and Guidelines. Version One; June 2000. <http://www.peoplesnetwork.gov.uk/nof/technicalstandards.html>

7. Oxford University. Policy on Computer Archiving Service. 1997. <http://www.oucs.ox.ac.uk/services/archiving/archive-policy.html>

8. Oxford University Computing Services. Preservation of the Electronic Assets of a University. 1997.
    <http://users.ox.ac.uk/~alex/hfs-AXIS-paper.html>

9. PADI. 'Storage'.
    <http://www.nla.gov.au/padi/topics/10.html>

10. TASI. Recommendations for Digital Preservation and Storage.
    <http://www.tasi.ac.uk/framework/collections/digital.html>

11. Van Bogart, J. (1995). Magnetic Tape Storage and Handling. Council on Library and Information Resources. (ISBN 1-887334-40-8).
    <http://www.clir.org/pubs/reports/pub54>

Preservation strategies – overviews and general guidance

1. Bearman, D. (1999). 'Reality and Chimeras in the Preservation of Electronic Records'. D-Lib Magazine. April 1999.
    <http://www.dlib.org/dlib/april99/bearman/04bearman.html>

2. Berthon, H. and Webb, C. (2000). 'The Moving Frontier: Archiving, Preservation and Tomorrow's Digital Heritage.' Paper presented at VALA 2000 – 10th VALA Biennial Conference and Exhibition, Melbourne, Victoria, 16-18 February 2000.
    <http://www.nla.gov.au/nla/staffpaper/hberthon2.html>

3. Hendley, T. (1998). Comparison of Methods & Costs of Digital Preservation. British Library Research and Innovation Report 106. London: The British Library. (ISBN 0 7123 9713 2)
    <http://www.ukoln.ac.uk/services/elib/papers/tavistock/hendley/hendley.html>

4. PADI. 'Digital Preservation Strategies'.
    <http://www.nla.gov.au/padi/topics/18.html>

Migration

5. Lawrence, G.W. et al. (2000). Risk Management of Digital Information: a File Format Investigation. Council on Library and Information Resources. June 2000. (ISBN 1-887334-78-5).
    <http://www.clir.org/pubs/abstract/pub93abst.html>

Emulation

6. CAMiLEON (Creative Archiving at Michigan and Leeds; Emulating the Old and the New) Project. Three-year NSF/JISC funded project commenced 1 October 1999. Further details online. Available from the Cedars website:
    <http://www.leeds.ac.uk/cedars>

7. Rothenberg, J. (2000). An Experiment in Using Emulation to Preserve Digital Publications. A report commissioned by the Koninklijke Bibliotheek (KB).
<http://www.kb.nl/nedlib/results/emulationpreservationreport.pdf>

8. Rothenberg, J. (1999). Avoiding Technological Quicksand: Finding a Viable Technical Foundation for Digital Preservation. Council on Library and Information Resources. January 1999. (ISBN 1-887334-63-7).
<http://www.clir.org/pubs/abstract/pub77.html>

Digital archaeology

9. Ross, S. and Gow, A. (1999). Digital Archaeology: Rescuing Neglected and Damaged Data Resources. British Library Research and Innovation Report 108. London, British Library, 1999.
<http://www.hatii.arts.gla.ac.uk/Projects/BrLibrary/rosgowrt.pdf>

Encapsulation

10. Heminger, A. R. and Robertson, S. B. (1998). 'Digital Rosetta Stone: A Conceptual Model for Maintaining Long-Term Access to Digital Documents.' ERCIM Workshop Proceedings No. 98-W003.
<http://www.ercim.org/publications/ws-proceedings/DELOS6/rosetta.pdf>

11. Reference Model for an Open Archival Information System (OAIS) Draft Recommendation for Space Data System Standards, of the Consultative Committee for Space Data Systems (CCSDS), CCSDS 650.0-R-1, May 1999.
<http://www.ccsds.org/RP9905/RP9905.html>

12. UPF (Universal Preservation Format). Home Page.
<http://info.wgbh.org/upf>

4.4 Metadata and Documentation

Archives, libraries and museums have always organised their collections to enable users to find the information they need more readily. This function is equally important in the digital environment where the speed of development and uptake of the Internet as a publishing medium has made the discovery of quality resources increasingly hazardous. Much work has been undertaken to develop standardised means of discovering online resources, most notably the fifteen elements represented in Dublin Core[1]. Increasingly, attention is being turned to the crucial role of documentation and metadata to facilitate the preservation of digital resources. Just as metadata to support resource discovery is not a new phenomenon, neither is the importance of documentation in preservation programmes:

"Documentation has always played a key role in preservation practice. This is not just a matter of academic interest: to manage collections or individual items one needs to know what one is dealing with. There are many instances where documentation provided the only information about processes that had been applied and might need to be corrected[2]."

While the concept is not new, there are factors which make documentation particularly critical for the continued viability of digital materials and they relate to fundamental differences between traditional and digital resources:

- **Technology** Digital resources are dependent on hardware and software to render them intelligible. There are many potential permutations of technical requirements which need to be documented so that decisions on appropriate preservation and access strategies may be made.
- **Change** The resource cannot be preserved as a single physical entity over time. The information it contains will need to be separated from its physical carrier and moved across different technological platforms if it is to remain accessible. This will inevitably produce changes which may or may not significantly affect the integrity and/or functionality of the resource. Documentation of actions taken on a resource and changes occurring as a result will provide a key to future managers and users of the resource.
- **Rights management** While traditional resources may or may not be copied as part of their preservation programme, digital resources must be copied if they are to remain accessible. Managers need to know that they have the right to copy for the purposes of preservation, what (if any) devices to control rights management, such as encryption, have been used, and what (if any) implications there are for controlling access.
- **Continuity** There will be many different decision-makers and operators and quite possibly different institutions influencing the management of digital materials across time. While traditional materials may be preserved by predominantly passive preventive preservation programmes, digital materials will be subject to repeated actions over a prolonged period of time.

- **Accountability** Documentation provides an audit trail of decisions affecting the long-term viability of the material.
- **Authenticity** Documentation may be the major, if not the only, means of reliably establishing the authenticity of material following changes.
- **Cost** It will be more complex and therefore more costly to maintain access to digital materials without documentation describing its technical characteristics.
- **Feasibility** It may not be possible to recreate the material without adequate documentation or at least not cost-effective to undertake complex restoration required as a result.
- **Future** Re-use.

Additional issues needing to be resolved are:

- **Costs** Given the complexity of digital materials and their requirements for preservation, it can be assumed that only a relatively limited set of essential preservation metadata can be automatically generated. This leads to questions of to what extent there may be overlapping needs of creators/owners and those taking on responsibility for long-term preservation of the resource:
  - What metadata needs to be/can be provided by creators/owners?
  - What will need to be/can be provided by the repository accepting preservation responsibility?
  - What is the most efficient and cost-effective means of gathering all necessary metadata and documentation prior to or simultaneously with ingest/acquisition?
  - What are the most efficient and effective means of ensuring that all necessary documentation and metadata is preserved along with the digital resource itself?

What still needs to be done?

While much progress has been made in defining what is required, actually ensuring that the information is readily and cost effectively accessible remains problematic. The technical environment changes so rapidly that software can become outdated before the repository undertakes responsibility. If a third party is undertaking responsibility for preservation the issue can become even more urgent when not even corporate memory is available to help unravel the puzzle.

Two recent studies have both drawn attention to the major obstacle of locating relevant hardware, software, and format documentation.

"Documentation for hardware and software initially ubiquitous when products are first released become increasingly difficult (and in some cases impossible) to locate over time. A concerted effort should be undertaken to collect documentation, including designs."[3]

An investigation undertaken by Cornell[4] found that successful migration programs were significantly hampered by the disparity between openly published file format specifications and the increasing use of modifications to the basic standard, the latter being rarely, if ever, publicly available. Their conclusion was that:

"There is a real and pressing need to establish reliable, sustained repositories of file format specifications, documentation, implementation guides, and related software. Cornell recommends the establishment of such repositories as a prerequisite to the development of an effective national strategy."[5]

Until these recommendations have been implemented, it will continue to be a hazardous and time consuming task successfully to preserve digital resources.

Organisational Activities

References

1. Dublin Core Metadata Initiative.
   <http://purl.org/DC>

2. National Library of Australia. Draft Preservation Metadata Set. October 1999. p. 2.
   <http://www.nla.gov.au/preserve/pmeta.html>

3. Ross, S. and Gow, A. (1999). Digital Archaeology: Rescuing Neglected and
   Damaged Data Resources. p. 6.
   <http://www.hatii.arts.gla.ac.uk/Projects/BrLibrary/rosgowrt.pdf >

4. Lawrence, G.W. et al. (2000). Risk Management of Digital Information: a File
   Format Investigation. Council on Library and Information Resources. June 2000.
   <http://www.clir.org/pubs/abstract/pub93abst.html>

5. 'Risk Management of Digital Information: a File Format Investigation'. RLG
   DigiNews 4 (3). 15 June 2000. p.14.
   <http://www.rlg.ac.uk/preserv/diginews/diginews4-3.html>

Exemplars and Further Reading

Documentation – standards and guidance

1. Data Documentation Initiative (DDI)
    <http://www.icpsr.umich.edu/DDI/codebook.html>

    This is an example of an initiative by a particular community, the social science research community, to "establish an international criterion and methodology for the content, presentation, transport and preservation of metadata about data sets in the social and behavioral sciences." Social science research has for many years pioneered the re-use of data emanating from research projects.

2. The Data Archive, University of Essex. Guide to Depositing Data. Guidelines for Documenting Data.
    <http://www.data-archive.ac.uk>

3. Arts and Humanities Data Service.
    <http://www.ahds.ac.uk>

    Individual service providers offer guidance on documentation, for example, the History Data Service: Guidelines for Documenting Data <http://hds.essex.ac.uk/guide.stm> and the Archaeology Data Service, Guidelines for Depositors Version 1.1 <http://ads.ahds.ac.uk/project/userinfo/deposit.html>. In addition, the Guides to Good Practice series also offer advice as well as guidance on why documentation is important. For example Creating Digital Resources for the Visual Arts: Standards and Good Practice. Section 4. Standards for Data Documentation <http://vads.ahds.ac.uk/guides/creating_guide/sect41.html> and Creating and Documenting Electronic Texts. Chapter 6: Documentation and Metadata. <http://ota.ahds.ac.uk/documents/creating/chap6.html>.

Metadata – developing standards

4. RLG Working Group on Preservation Issues of Metadata. Final Report. May 1998.
    <http://www.rlg.ac.uk/preserv/presmeta.html>

    The Working Group noted that to date the emphasis of metadata has been on resource discovery and retrieval. Taking two prominent metadata systems, Dublin Core and the Program for Cooperative Cataloguing's USMARC-based core record standard, the group specified those elements not covered by these two systems but important to serve the preservation needs of digital masters. The group confined itself to digital image files and recommended sixteen data elements for this category of digital resource.

5. Reference Model for an Open Archival Information System (OAIS) Draft Recommendation for Space Data System Standard. May 1999.
    <http://www.ccsds.org/RP9905/RP9905.html>
    This model aims to develop a common framework for all archives, digital and non digital. However of particular relevance and interest to the understanding of digital resources is the OAIS definition of Archival Information Packages (AIP's).

This recognises and identifies the range of elements required before a digital resource is useable and reinforces the fundamental differences between preserving digital and traditional resources. An AIP consists of both content information (both the data object and any Representation Information (RI) needed to render it intelligible) and Preservation Description Information (PDI), descriptive metadata which allows the essence of what the content information is to be understood indefinitely.

6. NEDLIB (Networked European Deposit Library)
    <http://www.konbib.nl/nedlib>

    This project has twelve partners consisting of deposit libraries, archives, and IT developers. Three publishers are also contributing to the project, which runs from January 1998 to December 2000. The main focus of NEDLIB has been on the technical aspects of digital preservation. NEDLIB has based its Deposit System for Electronic Publications (DSEP) on the OAIS model but has added a specific preservation module specifically to identify where "transformation processes" (i.e. migrations) take place.

7. Cedars Project Team and UKOLN. Metadata for Digital Preservation: the Cedars Project Outline Specification. Draft for Public Consultation. March 2000.
    <http://www.leeds.ac.uk/cedars>

    This document represents a major aspect of the work of Cedars in the development of a metadata framework which will enable the long-term preservation of digital resources. The outline indicates that it generally adheres to the metadata identified by the Reference Model for an Open Archival Information System (OAIS). The document "starts with the structure provided by the OAIS model and populates it with metadata elements chosen by practical investigation of archiving real digital resources, further refined by comments received from a selective consultation process." It also restricts itself to metadata required for preservation, rather than other processes.

8. National Library of Australia. Draft Preservation Metadata Set. October 1999.
    <http://www.nla.gov.au/preserve/pmeta.html>

    This has been developed as part of the NLA's plans for its digital collections. The introduction states that "There have been a number of efforts to develop metadata specifications and sets to support a wide variety of digital resources. Because of its pressing business needs to manage both 'born digital' and 'digital surrogate' collections, the National Library of Australia has tried to find, or if necessary develop, metadata models to accommodate both." The draft also emphasises that the metadata set is intended as a data output model, i.e. information required to manage digital collections, not necessarily what data should be entered, how it should be entered, by whom, and at what time. Like the Cedars specification, this document restricts itself to metadata required for preservation.

9. RLG/OCLC
    <http://www.rlg.ac.uk/pr/pr2000-oclc.html>

    On March 10 2000, RLG and OCLC agreed to combine forces to work towards creating infrastructures for digital archiving. The first steps towards this wider aim are collaboration on two working documents, one on characteristics of reliable archiving services and another on preservation metadata. The draft documents will be made available on both the RLG <http://www.rlg.ac.uk> and OCLC <http://www.oclc.org> and comments will be invited before final publication.

The above examples of work being undertaken in this area have all been based on practical experience and identified needs and show considerable progress is being made. Ongoing development is still needed, particularly for "published" digital resources. This is because a) it is impossible to predict precisely what will be required for heterogeneous digital resources, and b) as the above examples demonstrates, it is difficult to establish a standard set of elements satisfying the requirements of all institutions for all digital resources.

Record keeping metadata

10. National Archives of Australia. Recordkeeping Metadata Standard for Commonwealth Agencies. May 1999.
    <http://www.naa.gov.au/recordkeeping/control/rkms/summary.htm>

11. Bearman, David and Sochats, Ken. (1996). Metadata Requirements for Evidence. Pittsburgh, Pa: University of Pittsburgh School of Information Science.
    <http://www.lis.pitt.edu/~nhprc/BACartic.html>

12. Dollar, Charles. (1999). Authentic Electronic Records: Strategies for Long-Term Access. Chicago: Cohasset Associates. (ISBN 0-9700640-0-4).
    Appendix 7. Preservation Metadata Model.

4.5 Access

There has always been a strong link between preservation and access. The major objective of preserving the information content of traditional resources is so that they can remain accessible for future as well as current generations. The link is more explicit in the digital environment in that decisions on how to provide access and how to preserve a digital resource should be made, ideally, simultaneously. As well as the timing of decisions regarding preservation and access, there is also the fact that there is little point in preserving either the container or the bit stream of digital resources. To preserve access to them is also the key objective of digital preservation programmes but requires more active management throughout the lifecycle of the resource before it can be assured. While there is a strong link between preservation and access in terms of the overriding objective of a digital preservation programme, there is also a need to make a clear distinction between them. There may be a combination of technical, legal, and pragmatic reasons to separate the access copy from the preservation copy. This section looks at some of the implications for preservation which may need to be considered when developing an access strategy.

Storage and security

There needs to be both system and physical security if access is to be preserved over time. If the access copy is the only copy of a digital resource, then the danger of loss from theft or damage is clearly very high. In some instances, for example if large quantities of heterogeneous digital resources are being deposited with an institution, a pragmatic decision may have been made to maintain a single copy. If this approach is taken a risk assessment needs to be undertaken consisting of some of the following questions:

- Is it possible to obtain another copy of the resource from another source at any stage in the event of loss or damage? If No, make backup copy.
- Has a legal undertaking been made to preserve the resource? If Yes, make backup copy.
- Is the informational content in the resource rare or unique? If Yes, make backup copy.

See also **4.2** and **4.3**.

Legal

There are two main options for acquiring digital resources from external sources:

1. Via either purchase or legal requirement to deposit. This model is almost exactly analogous to the traditional model, except that additional negotiations regarding access and preservation need to be undertaken. Questions here relate to what access conditions have been permitted by the owners of the data. The ease with which digital resources can be copied and networked can be both a spur and an inhibitor to access as owners of the

data seek means of ensuring unauthorised access is not permitted. If responsibility has been taken to preserve the resource and the resource is subject to copyright, it may be necessary to restrict access either for a defined period of time and/or to standalone PCs. There is much debate on the most appropriate means of adapting legal frameworks developed for traditional materials to the digital environment. This handbook is primarily concerned with encouraging thought to be given to how to manage access sanctions which might be imposed, not whether or not they should exist.

2. License digital content for an agreed period of time. This is an increasingly prevalent model and one which is well suited to the digital environment where access is not dependent on physical custody. However, there are clearly issues regarding sustained access with, to use Ann Okerson's phrase, "the possibility of uncoupling ownership from access, the material object from its intellectual content"[1]. Much work has been done to try to streamline licenses, bringing obvious administrative benefits for both publishers and institutions. Model licences, such as the one developed by NESLI for electronic journals, state that publishers must continue to provide access to material previously paid for if a subscription is cancelled. However, it is important to be aware that, even when a supplier agrees to the concept of "perpetual access" this is not completely synonymous with digital preservation, though it does at least provide greater assurance of access for the foreseeable future (see also **2.3.3** and **3.4**).

Media
Depending on current and anticipated levels of use, it may be more practical to have copies stored offline, nearline, or online. What policies and procedures need to be in place to decide which of these is most appropriate, and how the resource can be preserved regardless of where it is stored?

Technical
The large file sizes associated with uncompressed formats may make access time unacceptably slow. Similarly some formats may be more suited to presentation and therefore access but not necessarily appropriate for long-term preservation.

References

1. Okersen, Ann. (1992) in University Libraries and Scholarly Communication: A Study Prepared for the Andrew W Mellon Foundation. p. xxiii. <http://etext.lib.virginia.edu/reports/mellon/mellon.html>

Exemplars and Further Reading

Many of the references cited in further reading sections elsewhere in the handbook, in particular those in **4.1** also include sections relevant to access. In addition, the following are references for model licences:

1. ECUP (European Copyright User Platform) Licensing Issues.
   <http://www.eblida.org/ecup/licensing/lic.htm>

2. Licensingmodels.com.
   <http://www.licensingmodels.com>

3. NESLI (National Electronic Site Licensing Initiative).
   <http://www.nesli.ac.uk>

5. Media and Formats

Intended primary audience

Operational managers and staff in repositories, publishers and other data creators, third party service providers.

Assumed level of knowledge of digital preservation

Novice to Intermediate.

Purpose

To outline the range of options available when creating digital materials and some of the major implications of selection. To point to more detailed sources of advice and guidance. To indicate areas where it is necessary to maintain an active technology watch.

5.1 Media

It is important to have an understanding of the various media for storage because they require different software and hardware equipment for access, and have different storage conditions and preservation requirements. They also have varying suitability according to the storage capacity required, and preservation or access needed.

Although it is very easy to focus on the traditional conservation of the physical artefact, it is important to recognise that most electronic media will be threatened by obsolescence of the hardware and software to access them. This often occurs long before deterioration of media (which have been subject to appropriate storage and handling) becomes a problem. However, appropriate selection, storage and handling of media is still essential to any preservation strategy (see **4.3**).

Obsolescence of previous storage media has occurred in rapid succession. In floppy disks alone we have seen a progression from 8 in to 5.25 in and then 3.5 in formats, with each change leading to rapid discontinuation of previous formats and difficulty in obtaining or maintaining access devices for them.

Mass storage devices have a long history and this section deals only with the magnetic and optical storage media which are in widespread or recent use. An interesting historical account of "new media" can be found in the PRO Preservation Guide series[1].

Magnetic media

Consist of a variety of magnetic media and containers including a range of magnetic tapes (e.g. reels, cartridges and cassettes) and disks (e.g. hard disks, floppy disks). They all utilise the magnetic properties of metallic materials suspended in a non-magnetic mixture on a substrate or backing material.

This provides a versatile and cheap storage medium and both the storage capacity and the ability to retain the magnetic charges holding the data have increased substantially in recent years. The method of construction and storing the data also point to potential weaknesses of magnetic media.

You should ensure appropriate storage away from strong magnetic fields as these may alter the media and lead to data loss (e.g. electrical equipment and motors). Damage from magnetic fields is rare and the media normally has to be in very close proximity (<50 mm) for this to occur. Tape enclosures or packing with a space clearance of 50 mm around the media is recommended for use during transportation and transfer.

Clean operating conditions and environments will reduce the scope for damage to media and devices. The high density of storage and the close proximity of device heads to the media mean even small particles such as smoke or other debris can lead to data loss.

Handling and use of magnetic storage media should be minimised to reduce wear, or refreshment cycles implemented (as recommended by the manufacturer) to replace media on a more frequent basis reflecting the levels of use.

Poor environmental storage may also lead to oxidation of the ferromagnetic material or problems with the "binding" layer or substrate materials. Recommendations for the storage environment of magnetic media are provided in **4.3**.

Magnetic media are constantly evolving and in addition to fundamental changes in devices manufacturers often undertake an almost constant evolution of production processes. Although the reliability of magnetic media has improved over recent years it is important to be aware that faults in manufacture can occur and to make appropriate checks of new media when purchased. Media should also be of high quality and purchased from reputable brands and suppliers. As an additional safeguard archive copies can be made to comparable magnetic media purchased from different suppliers to guard against faults introduced into products or batches of the product by the manufacturers.

In addition to the magnetic media themselves it is important that attention is paid to the recording and access devices such as tape drives. These should be of good quality and well-maintained. Problems with the access devices e.g. head/media crashes are one of the most common cases of damage to magnetic storage media. It may also be desirable to write archive copies from different devices and software to protect data form malfunctioning devices or software.

Optical media

Optical storage media such as CD-ROM (Compact Disc – Read Only Memory), CD-R (Compact Disc -Recordable), and DVD-ROM (Digital Versatile Disc – Read Only Memory) use laser light to read from a data layer. In CD-ROM this data layer consists of a series of pits and plateaux in a metallic coating over a plastic disk. A clear acrylic coating is applied to the metallic layer to protect it from scratches and corrosion. CD-R employs a dye layer which is light sensitive as the data layer. Data is written to and read back using laser light. The use of light sensitive dyes means CD-Rs are less stable than CD-ROMs and more concerns have been raised over their use as archival media[2]. As with magnetic media there is considerable diversity in

Media and Formats

practice and production of CD-R and greater care is needed in selecting high quality media from reputable suppliers for archival purposes. DVD-ROM is a more recent optical storage medium with capacity to store 4.7-18 Gb.

Optical disks are an increasingly popular method of storage. The device reader is not in contact with the disk and mechanical failure is less likely to lead to data loss than damage to the disk itself through poor handling or storage. Disks should not be flexed or their surfaces marked or abraded e.g. through use of a sharp pen or pencil for labelling. The manufacturer's recommendation for marking should be followed.

As with magnetic media, optical media have been subject to a constant process of evolution and changes in manufacture. The quality of the media, a reputable source, and appropriate handling and storage environment (see **4.3**) will all affect its longevity.

Media life

Media should be refreshed on a regular cycle within the lifetime for archival storage identified by the manufacturer or independent sources such as the US National Media Laboratory. Sample generic figures for lifetimes of media under various temperature and humidity levels assuming optimal use (no or very infrequent access) and environmental conditions (stable and free of contaminants, u-v light and strong magnetic fields) are given in the figure below. It should be noted that the life of specific media will be dependent on the quality of manufacture. Media life will vary between specific products and dates (e.g. the earliest CDs will be more experimental in manufacture than current versions; branded "Gold" CDs will have longer life than cheaper standard products).

Figure 7
Sample Generic Figures for Lifetimes of Media

Device	25RH 10°C	30RH 15°C	40RH 20°C	50RH 25°C	50RH 28°C
D3 magnetic tape	50 years	25 years	15 years	3 years	1 year
DLT magnetic tape cartridge	75 years	40 years	15 years	3 years	1 year
CD/DVD	75 years	40 years	20 years	10 years	2 years
CD-ROM	30 years	15 years	3 years	9 months	3 months

After Dollar[3], NML[4] and PRO[5]

5.2 File Format and Standards

As with storage media there is a diverse range of formats (e.g. Word, TIFF) in common use. The purpose of this section is not to provide a detailed or exhaustive list of current formats for different media types but to draw attention to the broader implications of file formats for their application, and implications for preservation. There are a number of excellent sources of more detailed advice on file formats and these are detailed in the further reading to the chapter.

File formats are subject to similar rapid obsolescence and evolution and the process of selection and assessment of options for preservation is largely one of risk reduction. Use of file formats which have been well documented, have undergone thorough testing and are non-proprietary and usable on different hardware and software platforms minimises the frequency of migration and reduces the risk and costs in their preservation. Similarly utilising formats which have been widely adopted minimises risk as it is more likely that migration paths will be provided by the manufacturers and a degree of "backward compatibility" will be available between versions of the file format as it evolves. It is important to note that backward compatibility is rarely maintained for more than one or two previous versions and that the "window of opportunity" to migrate is therefore relatively brief.

Although such non-proprietary formats can be selected for many resource types this is not universally the case. For many new areas and applications, e.g. Geographical Information Systems or Virtual Reality only proprietary formats are available. In such cases a crucial factor will be the export formats supported to allow data to be moved out of (or into) these proprietary environments.

It is advisable for institutions where possible to identify file formats which are preferred for archival storage and to seek deposits in that form wherever a choice of formats exist. Some institutions have also identified and distinguished between preferred, acceptable and unacceptable formats for transfer to the institution, for archival storage once in the institution's care, and formats which can be provided for users. Narrowing the range of file formats handled streamlines the management process and reduces preservation costs. It will also reduce the ongoing cost of software licences required by the institution (see also **4.2** and **4.3.1**). In considering storage and preservation it is helpful to recognise that it can be a desirable strategy to distinguish between formats (or versions) used for archiving and access on the basis of different requirements e.g. it would be appropriate to store a high resolution image as a TIFF master file (archival format), but to distribute the image as a JPEG file (access format) of smaller size for transmission over a network. It would not be appropriate to store the JPEG image as both the access and archival format because of the irretrievable data loss this would involve.

The speed with which many file formats evolve and the degree to which even well documented standard formats can be extended by proprietary additions or modified/adapted for specific applications by users also has significant implications for preservation, and in particular for good preservation metadata and system documentation (see **4.4**).

5.3 Compression and Encryption

File compression algorithms can substantially reduce file sizes and have been widely used in document or image transmission. Compression can either be lossless or lossy (with data loss but often higher levels of compression). Although appropriate in many cases for access and user copies, compression adds additional complexity to the preservation process and is normally not recommended for the storage of archival files. With current increases in storage capacity and reducing costs it is also less necessary. For some very large files e.g. digitised video, compressed formats may be the only viable option however for capture, storage and transmission.

In a similar way encryption is increasingly prevalent either to ensure that sensitive data is read only by the recipient or to ensure a digital product can only be used by an authorised user. Encryption also adds to the complexity of the preservation process and should be avoided if possible for archival copies. This may require strict implementation of physical and system security procedures for the archive of unencrypted files, or archival access to encryption keys.

5.4 Technology Watch

An implication of the rapid evolution of storage media and file formats and the risks of technology obsolescence is the necessity of maintaining a register of hardware and software capacity in the institution and preservation metadata to enable a formal process of "technology watch". The degree to which this will be necessary will vary according to the degree of uniformity or control over formats and media that can be exercised by the institution. Those with little control over media and formats received and a high degree of diversity in their holdings will find this function essential. For most other institutions the IS strategy should seek to develop corporate standards so that everybody uses the same software and versions and is migrated to new versions as the products develop.

Deborah Woodyard[6] describes how preservation metadata was gathered by the National Library of Australia to determine what hardware and software were required by its digital holdings. A list of hardware and software available in the NLA was also developed and maintained. This is used to flag potential changes in technology and the requirement to retain hardware and software still needed by the collection until migration has occurred.

Failure to implement an effective technology watch or IS strategy incorporating this will risk potential loss of access to digital holdings and higher costs. It may be possible to re-establish access through a process of "digital archaeology" (see **4.3.2**) but this is likely to be expensive compared to pre-emptive strategies.

A retrospective survey of digital holdings and a risk assessment and action plan may be a necessary first step for many institutions, prior to implementing a technology watch.

Good preservation metadata in a computerised catalogue identifying the storage medium (3.5 in floppy disk, DVD etc.), the necessary hardware (IBM PC compatible, Apple Mac), operating system (Windows 95, NT, Dos 3.0 etc.) and software (e.g. Word 6) will enable a technology watch strategy.

5.5   Summary Recommendations

Media
- Keep store and access areas free of smoke, dust, dirt and other contaminants.
- Store magnetic media away from strong magnetic fields.
- Transport magnetic media in enclosures with space clearances of 50 mm.
- Store in a cool, dry, stable and secure environment (see **4.3**).
- Acclimatise media before use.
- Use high quality media and devices.
- Keep access devices well maintained and clean.
- Do not place labels on optical disks and/or mark using a pen or pencil.
- Follow manufacturers' recommendations for labelling.
- Minimise handling and use of archival media and/or record number of accesses/use and implement appropriate refreshing.
- Write archival copies from different devices and software.
- Make archive copies to comparable media purchased from different suppliers.

File formats
- Use "open" non-proprietary, well-documented file formats wherever possible.

- Alternatively utilise file formats which are well-developed, have been widely adopted and are de facto standards in the marketplace.
- Identify formats acceptable for the purposes of transfer, storage and distribution to users (these may be distinct).
- Minimise the number of file formats to be managed as far as is feasible/desirable.
- Do not use encryption or compression for archival files if possible.

Technology watch

- Undertake a retrospective survey of digital holdings, a risk assessment and action plan.
- Implement a process of technology watch and/or implement procedures for standardisation and changes in technology in your IS strategy.
- Maintain a list of hardware/software available within the institution and use this to flag implications for technology change and hardware/software replacement/retention.
- Ensure you have good preservation metadata in a computerised catalogue which can form the basis for technology watch and monitoring.
- Consider "digital archaeology" to retrieve access to data in obsolete formats.

References

1. Farley, J. (1999). An Introduction to Archival Materials; new media (PRO Preservation Guide series). Available free from the PRO.

2. Ross, S. and Gow, A. (1999). Digital Archaeology: Rescuing Neglected and Damaged Data Resources. British Library Research and Innovation Report 108. London, The British Library, 1999.
<http://www.hatii.arts.gla.ac.uk/Projects/BrLibrary/rosgowrt.pdf>

3. Dollar, C. (2000). Authentic Electronic Records: Strategies for Long-Term Access. Chicago: Cohasset Associates. (ISBN 0-9700640-0-4).

4. Work of Dr J. van Bogart for National Media Laboratory (NML) United States previously available online at <http://www.nml.org>. Site available through search-engine caches June 2001. Please note as the handbook goes to press a new publication, Data Storage Technology Assessment 2000 by Koichi Sadashige for the National Media Laboratory and the National Technology Alliance will be available on CD from the NML.

5. PRO 1999. A Digital Preservation Strategy for the PRO. November 1999.

6. Woodyard, D. (1999). 'Practical Advice for Preserving Publications on Disk'. Presented at Information Online and Ondisc '99, Darling Harbour, Sydney, 21 January 1999.
<http://www.nla.gov.au/nla/staffpaper/woodyard2.html>

Media and Formats

Exemplars and Further Reading

1. Beagrie, N. and Greenstein, D. (1998). Managing Digital Collections: AHDS Policies, Standards and Practices. Consultation Draft. December 1999. <http://www.ahds.ac.uk/policies.htm>

   Section 2.9.2 Technical Standards, provides a summary of preferred formats recommended by AHDS service providers. Further details are available in individual Guides to Good Practice.

2. DLM Forum (1997). Guidelines on Best Practice for Using Electronic Information. <http://europa.eu.int/ISPO/dlm/documents/gdlines.pdf>

   Chapter 5, Short- and long-term preservation of electronic information, offers advice on data storage media (including advice on storage conditions) and file formats. The latter general advice is "Best practice is to decide on a common set of standards from the outset to make it easier to circulate information. Preferably the same formats should be used for both short-term and long-term preservation". Both storage media and file formats are grouped into families, with examples of the major types in each.

3. Frey, F. (2000). File Formats for Digital Masters. <http://www.rlg.ac.uk/visguides/visguide5.html>

   One of five guides commissioned by DLF and CLIR and published with RLG. This guide provides steps in how to select file formats for digital masters, selecting those based on a combination of performance and durability.

4. National Library of Australia. (1999). First Steps in Preserving Digital Publications. <http://www.nla.gov.au/pres/epupam.html>

5. PADI. This is highly recommended as providing comprehensive links to relevant resources. Relevant sections available online include:
   magnetic media at: <http://www.nla.gov.au/padi/topics/59.html>
   optical disks at: <http://www.nla.gov.au/padi/topics/53.html>
   physical formats at: <http://www.nla.gov.au/padi/topics/52.html>

6. TASI. Framework webpages are highly recommended as a resource and are available online at: <http://www.tasi.ac.uk/framework/framework.html>

   Includes general advice on selecting file formats for images.

7. van Bogart, John (1995). Magnetic Tape Storage and Handling. Council on Library and Information Resources. (ISBN 1-887334-40-8). <http://www.clir.org/pubs/reports/pub54>

8. Dale, R. (1999). File compression Strategies Discussion at ALA. RLG DigiNews February 15 1999. <http://www.rlg.ac.uk/preserv/diginews/diginews3-1.html>

Topic Index

Topic Index